T0067424

Alchemical Inheritance

Embracing What Is, Manifesting What Becomes

T ESS   K EEHN ,   M .   S .

W ITH H. H ARRIS W ILLCOCKSON
E DITED BY M ARY E LLEN R YDER , M. D IV .

BALBOA.
PRESS
A DIVISION OF HAY HOUSE

Balboa Press books may be ordered through booksellers or by contacting:

Balboa Press
A Division of Hay House
1663 Liberty Drive
Bloomington, IN 47403
www.balboapress.com
1 (877) 407-4847

Because of the dynamic nature of the Internet, any web addresses or links contained in this book may have changed since publication and may no longer be valid. The views expressed in this work are solely those of the author and do not necessarily reflect the views of the publisher, and the publisher hereby disclaims any responsibility for them.

The author of this book does not dispense medical advice or prescribe the use of any technique as a form of treatment for physical, emotional, or medical problems without the advice of a physician, either directly or indirectly. The intent of the author is only to offer information of a general nature to help you in your quest for emotional and spiritual well-being. In the event you use any of the information in this book for yourself, which is your constitutional right, the author and the publisher assume no responsibility for your actions.

Any people depicted in stock imagery provided by Thinkstock are models, and such images are being used for illustrative purposes only.
Certain stock imagery © Thinkstock.

Print information available on the last page.

ISBN: 978-1-5043-4346-6 (sc)
ISBN: 978-1-5043-4347-3 (e)

Library of Congress Control Number: 2015917505

Balboa Press rev. date: 11/19/2015

Disclaimer

Alchemical Inheritance is a unique blend of personal experience and therapeutic insight written by (Harris) Tess Keehn, who once worked as a California Licensed Marriage and Family Therapist and currently holds only an inactive license. She no longer diagnoses or treats mental illness. As such, this book, its associated websites and the opinions expressed therein should not be understood as counseling advice or recommendations.

Every person is on a different journey in their life. What has helped Ms. Keehn overcome some of the obstacles on her particular path may not work for you. Please do not assume that her successes will be your solutions. You must decide what is best for you and your life's path.

Always consult a trained mental health professional before making any decision regarding treatment choice or changes in your treatment. Never discontinue treatment or medication without first consulting your physician, clinician or therapist. If you are feeling like you want to do harm to yourself or others, please seek immediate assistance by calling 911, talking in real time with your physician or clinician or visiting the emergency department of the nearest hospital.

The information offered by this book and the associated websites is designed to support, not replace, the relationship that exists between an interested reader and his/her physician, clinician or mental health care professional. The mention of any program or provider in this book is not to be construed as recommendation for treatment.

Dedicated to

My husband, Michael,
whose alchemical love
continues to transform me.

Photo by TRENTONBAHR.COM

Contents

Foreword

To be witness to a person's spiritual and emotional life and its unfolding before one's eyes is usually reserved for psychotherapists in the privacy and confidentiality of the consulting room.

With Tess Keehn's book, however, we are like the therapist - a witness and emotional participant in her life and its continuing unfoldment.

Alchemical Inheritance is a rare book written with both the openness of a client and the discerning eye of a skilled professional psychotherapist. Tess Keehn is both.

The spiritual truths and "lesson" of her life are allowed to emerge through compassionate detail. Murder, alcoholism, suicide, beauty, inspiration and love are all shared with precision and gentleness. Unlike the majority of spiritual and psychological journey accounts, *Alchemical Inheritance* is not sensational or grandiose. Tess is not trying to portray herself as heroic, wise or even finished on her journey.

Alchemical Inheritance, like Tess herself, is real, accessible and humbly inspiring. Are you looking for an account of how an actual person wakes up to their life? With ideas and insights that we can use ourselves?

Keep reading!

Lama Yeshe Jinpa
(Stephen Bryant Walker)

MiddleWayHealth.com
Middle Way Health
Sacramento, California

Preface

A lchemical Inheritance* has been over 20 years in the making. Actually, it's been more like 59 years. I lived this life before I could write about it.

When I was 37 years old, underemployed in an administrative assistant position for a large corporation, I had job stability but no job satisfaction. When the notion of becoming a counselor first worked its way into the part of my mind that could entertain such a thought, the *other* part of my mind immediately chimed in with all its considerations, negativity and fear: "It's going to take two years! How can you afford graduate school? How will you ever be able to support yourself while studying full-time? You're not going to be any good as a counselor! Who do you think you are to ponder an advanced degree?"

"The time is going to go by anyway!" I countered. "I can just take a step in that direction and see what happens about money! I am definitely smart enough to earn a Master's degree! So just shut up!"

Besides, I *can't* be working *here* when I turn 40!

In my 20-year career as a licensed mental health provider in and around Sacramento, California, I have worked with people of all ages to resolve concerns and self-defeating behaviors of all colors, textures and flavors. From my beginnings as an art therapist in the Children's Bereavement Art Group, through private practice, work as an Employee Assistance Program counselor and then in the department of psychiatry at a local health maintenance organization, I discovered two things about people.

First: the motivation for change usually comes from the pain of discontent. Second: the ability to change is usually funded by a willingness to be wrong – to realize we have arrived at mistaken beliefs about ourselves, others and the world in which we live. The correction of those errors of perception is usually the foundation of the value gained in therapy. Not everyone is able to get to this place. So, sadly, not everyone will benefit from therapy. Or at least perhaps not on their first pass.

I have always wanted to tell the story of my family's tragedy that, I believe, shaped my mother so dramatically. I waited these 20 years to complete this book because it took me that long to fully comprehend it (and her) myself.

Few, if any, of us arrive at adulthood without baggage we've collected along the way. Usually some of it was provided by our parents. Nowhere is it written, however, that we have to carry those bags throughout our lives. That is a choice. It's a choice we would not have if those parents had not brought us here to live our lives. Moving through whatever healing is necessary to arrive at the gratitude for life itself is a worthy effort.

This book will probably call to you if, wherever you are, you don't want to be *there* at your next milestone birthday!

Acknowledgements

T his book would not exist if not for the love and support of my amazingly kind and grounded husband, Michael.

I only found him because I found the Unity church and had already begun to allow the power of positive thinking to awaken my inner quest.

Reverends Faith and Michael Moran so graciously embodied those principles and provided healthful role modeling for becoming the best possible expression of myself (as they were themselves.) The church they founded, Spiritual Life Center, continues to spread light and peace as a beacon of higher consciousness in our world.

I hold deep gratitude for my dear friends who read drafts and provided feedback: Jennifer Helm, Deborah Laughlin, Suzanne Joy-Livingston, Reverend Janee Artero Marth, Christine Jones, Susan Riegel, Anita Hansen, Sharon Ankrum and Michael Keehn.

I am forever indebted to Reverend Mary Ellen Ryder for her brilliant editing and unparalleled support during the gestation of this work and then the labor of preparing for publication. Her coaching empowered me to meet my 20-year deadline. I am changed for the better because of that.

Abundant thanks are also due to Reverend Becca Costello for her invaluable editorial contributions and support.

Dr. Michael Kwiker and the capable staff at Health Associates in Sacramento provided me with the correct diagnosis and treatment of adrenal fatigue which empowered me to focus on the light at the end of the tunnel in order to emerge well and whole.

My adopted family of Keehn sisters and their parents took me in and loved me generously from the start. I hope I've loved them back even half as well.

Jamie, Margaret and G.W. guided and nurtured me all the time I was that littlest member of our family. You are steeped in love and drenched in my gratitude.

Also forever in my heart are my parents whose love inspired me into being: for Helen who gave all she could and Roy who believed in me when it mattered most.

Introduction

All the world's a stage. And all the men
and women merely players.
~Shakespeare

D oes life live us or do we live life?
     Until my transformational experience in an EST-inspired workshop, in the mid-1980s, life lived me. It was just a series of things that happened to me. I had little direction and no sense of my ability – let alone response-ability – to impact the course of events that seemed to randomly steer my life. Ever since the moment of my spiritual awakening in ONE, life has beckoned me forward, inviting me to claim the wheel and pilot myself onward, moving incrementally more deeply into full acceptance that only I am accountable for my choices. Once I accepted that invitation, I began to live life.

From the moment I entered into that contract with myself, I began to see that life had always been ready to provide me with a deep well of nurturance and opportunities to heal. Daring to draw up buckets from that well has both strengthened and angered me. Yet the deeper I drew, the deeper I healed. This well nurtures me still as I continue to move through the precious years granted me in this lifetime – years to drink in all that life offers, to allow it to shape me into the person I am always becoming and to share the gifts I have been given. There were times when the well seemed dry; others when the bucket was so very heavy that I wasn't sure I could raise it. Yet something kept me going, placing one hand over the other on the rope to draw up the resources with all their beauty and grief for this journey of living.

I am certainly not alone in my struggles. Many others have written heroic accounts of the enlivening human ability to prevail even in the face of staggering trauma, pain and deprivation. By comparison, my journey into life was made much easier because of the privileged family into which I was born. My mother's family had been in the ranching business for three generations while it was still possible to amass great fortunes that way. They were already wealthy when oil was discovered under their thousands of acres of grassland. At age 24, I was due to inherit almost one million dollars. By age 29, I had witnessed most of that wealth disintegrate into the economic recession of the 1980s melting into failed investments in oil and gas, real estate and commodities futures. I had a Bachelor's degree, no real direction in life and only a fading memory of having been told I would never have to work.

The course change I experienced at age 29 has been my true inheritance – an inheritance of far greater value than ranchland and mineral rights. This has been my Alchemical Inheritance – the challenge (or invitation) to take something seemingly without value and transform it into a gleaming vat of precious metal. I wouldn't trade that course change now for anything.

Affluence makes the way easier but can have its own drawbacks as well. The difference, it has been said, between rich depressed people and poor ones is that the rich ones know that money cannot cure depression by making a person happy and fulfilled. The security of enough money to meet one's needs is clearly a benefit to anyone suffering from emotional or psychological troubles. It sends the wolf away from the door; stress levels immediately settle down. However, just as the requirement to work when we are not able is a stressor, the absence of purpose that can come with an unearned income is often itself a cause of great despair.

We humans are generously equipped, programmed and destined to create value with our lives. To be sure, wealth allows many diversions from the facts and circumstances at the root of despair.

All of the numbing agents are more available (but not exclusively so) to people with money - alcohol, recreational drugs, over-spending, over-eating - to name just a few. But diversion is not resolution. Troubles left unaddressed will fester until finally the pain becomes so great that something must be done. At that point, the rich person and the poor person stand on the same threshold, with Life demanding they take action to heal and thereby change the course of their existence.

We have all heard the stories of devastating and unspeakable horrors that children have endured. These horrors are not restricted to any particular socio-economic sector. So often these stories are told by the wounded who have risen above their histories to become incredibly empowered people. Such are the gifts of introspection, accountability and forgiveness. I do not pretend that my circumstances are equivalent to the more horrific stories. Despite trauma and abandonment, there was a stable floor beneath me in the family where I grew up.

The commonality, though, is present in the fact that intense loss, severe grief and debilitating trauma affect so many people even in our prosperous country. And how much worse must it be in corners of the world without civil rights, social services and due process? Emotional injuries left unhealed stunt the growth of souls who were granted this privilege of living in a human body in order to share their gifts with the world. Too often these gifts remain dormant, waiting for the emotional debris of victimization to be cleared. Only out of that clarity can the healed person share the full impact of who s/he is. In a world facing so many challenges, we need every human to be free to make their insightful contributions to answers and solutions for a better world.

The intention of this book is to offer the wisdom I have gleaned from the process of healing grief at depth. If my story empowers even two people to begin the journey to find a way home from the dark forest of a pained and grieving heart, then the lovely labor of writing it will have been worth it. Much of my self-reflection and healing has been influenced by the principles of the New Thought

Christianity movement that began in the late nineteenth century with the emergence of Transcendentalist thought. These gave rise to the development of the Unity Church and other ministries. I've also looked to the East to hone practices of meditation and prayer that have been cornerstones of my healing. While I have great respect for scientific method, I have borrowed hungrily from mystical ways of seeing, believing and understanding our spiritual natures. I am grateful for all of the world religions that teach love, and for those religions yet to emerge as humanity and perhaps consciousness itself continue to evolve.

Thank you for taking the time to read the stories of these three generations of Helens. My heartfelt wish is that they inspire you to take action to move yourself and your loved ones toward greater emotional wellbeing, more vibrant physical health and an increasingly harmonious relationship with our world and whatever you deem to be Higher Power.

I have changed some names out of courtesy for those I knew too long ago to contact to ask their permission to share stories involving them.

I have pieced together the beginning of this story from the oral history of my family and from relevant newspaper articles of the day. I began the newspaper research in about 1998. The Internet for personal use was new and I had no access to it at home. Through an inter-library loan, I was able to view the San Angelo Standard Times and the Houston Post microfiche records and to read the articles published during the period of the crime that is detailed in Chapter One. The Houston Post has become the Houston Chronicle and my searching concluded that the Houston Post archives are not readily available online. Other regional and national newspapers covered this sensational crime, but I limited my research to these two, more local papers.

The first three chapters contain over one hundred footnotes, almost all of which cite the sources of quotes from those two newspapers. I wanted the newspapers to tell the story in the way it unfolded in 1955. My intention is that my own feelings about those events can thereby stand out, separate from the story itself. I cite other sources as well and later chapters contain a few footnotes with explanatory information. All of these references are listed in Endnotes.

The crime involves a man by the name of Harry Leonard Washburn. This is not the Harry Washburn who served as a well-respected civic leader in the city of Houston for many years. That revered man has a tunnel named after him. Please be aware that I know of no familial connection between the two men and, in fact, I believe there is none.

There are two writers to this story, hence the two names listed as author. I am both of these people. Or at least I was. Born Helen Harris Willcockson, I chose to change my name in my late thirties when I began to know more clearly who I am. I became Tess when I started graduate school to receive my training as a mental health counselor. I married about one year after earning my Master's degree and, both personally and professionally, became Tess Keehn. Even as the name is clear, my personal and spiritual growing continues. I know the same is true for you. May you encounter a wealth of wonders, blessings and wise ones on your journey to your Self.

Harris Family Genogram

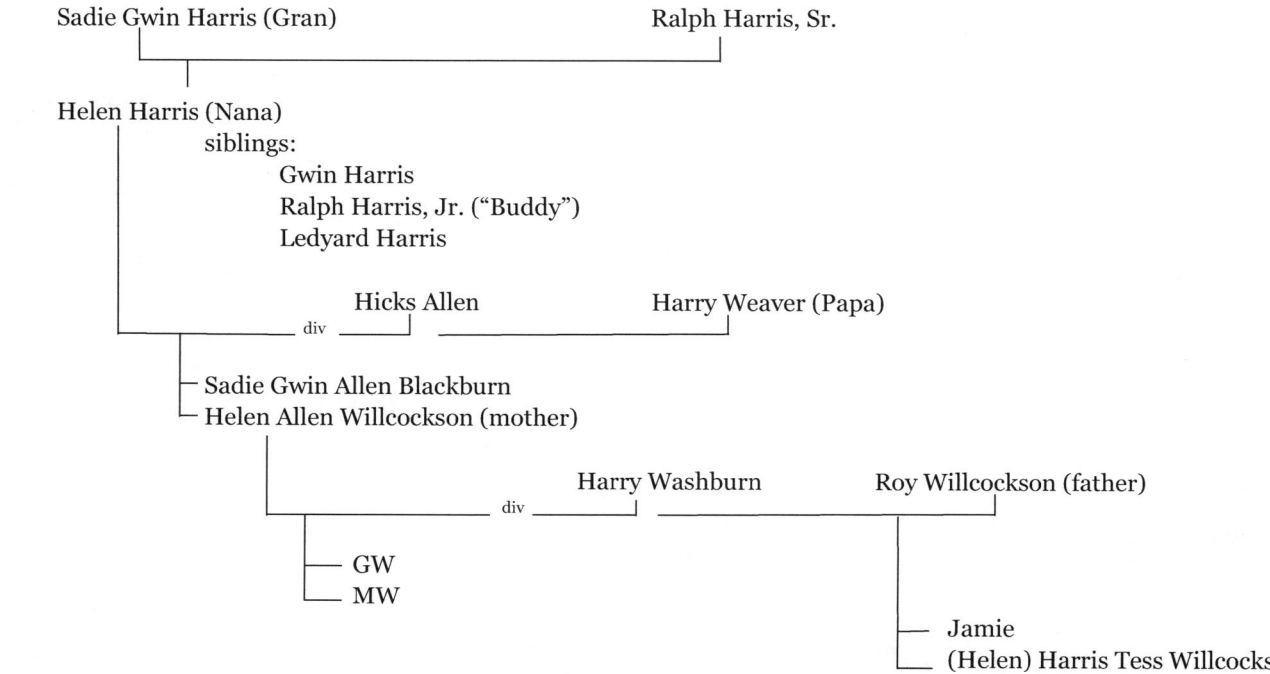

Sadie Gwin Harris (Gran)   Ralph Harris, Sr.

Helen Harris (Nana)
    siblings:
        Gwin Harris
        Ralph Harris, Jr. ("Buddy")
        Ledyard Harris

          Hicks Allen   Harry Weaver (Papa)
    div

    Sadie Gwin Allen Blackburn
    Helen Allen Willcockson (mother)

          Harry Washburn   Roy Willcockson (father)
      div

      GW
      MW

             Jamie
             (Helen) Harris Tess Willcockson Keehn

CHAPTER ONE

Crime

A man ain't poor for not havin' money.
He's poor from wantin' too much.
~Elmer Kelton

I wonder what she was doing when she heard her mother had been killed. I know my mother, Helen, was in Billings, Montana, married to my father by then. (Her two children from her first marriage were living in Texas with their father.) She was probably spending time with her new little boy, my brother Jamie. He would have been about a year and a half old, tow-headed and getting into things. It was January; they could have been out playing in the snow when the call came.

I can almost see the phone ringing and ringing with no one there to hear. It was 1955, long before touch tones and answering machines. I imagine her stepfather or her sister would have been trying to reach her to give her the tragic news. The phone was most likely black, with the circle on the face for dialing. My father tells me the house was furnished with the tasteful gifts my mother had received from her friends for her first wedding in Texas before she divorced and then met my father. I suppose my mother, Helen, got the call and then phoned my father to tell him. But it may have been the other way around. My mother was a bit fragile even then; her stepfather or sister might well have thought it better for her to hear the news in person from her husband. My father, Roy, would most likely have been at work, coming up with better ways to interpret data in order to locate oil underneath the Dakotas, Wyoming and Montana. My Aunt Sadie Gwin told me many years later that my father had invented something of great interest in oil exploration and that, in return, he was given a promotion. My father said she was being overly generous in her memory of things and that he never actually invented anything. He was a smart man and, I assume, diligent and good at his job. In 1957 or so, he *was* given the promotion that moved our family to Tehran, Iran - far from his Oklahoma roots and a grand adventure for this Tulsa, son-of-a-widow turned Westinghouse scholar and Geophysicist. Roy was far too modest to elaborate on any of that. In Iran, the Shah was in charge and Americans were welcome.

Our move to Iran came about four years after the news of Nana's death. Nana was my mother's mother, born Helen Harris. Nana named my mother, her second child, after herself. Then I was named after them both. The family history is a little confusing due to the repetition of some names - like Helen and Sadie Gwin - and also because of a Southern tradition of using last names (surnames) as middle names for offspring. My Nana married Hicks Allen and became Helen Harris Allen. My Aunt Sadie Gwin was born first, then my mother about two years later.

Nana had been living on the Harris family ranch in Coke County in West Texas for several years prior to her death. She had inherited the property when her father, Ralph Harris, died in 1943. She and my grandfather, Hicks, divorced after the Harris family tried for several years to make a rancher out of Hicks. They set the couple up on good ranchland, not knowing that West Texas was in the beginning of a seven year drought cycle that would destroy even some of the best, most established ranchers. Hicks was an engineer at heart and I think it must have been the strain of trying to be something he wasn't that drove the marriage apart.

Nana married again and became Mrs. Harry Weaver. Mr. Weaver was an architect, fairly well known in the state, with buildings to his credit, primarily in Houston. We knew him as Papa. He had married my grandmother when my mother and aunt were still children so he had a hand in raising them. Some years later, when he retired, he went with Nana to live on that Coke County ranch, just north of San Angelo, Texas. He designed and built the ranch house there. One of my earliest memories involves naptime on cots with a warm West Texas breeze moving through that house. I was about three and we had just returned from Iran because my father had retired from the oil business to settle in San Angelo.

The ranch house had a large barbecue area out back, toward the slope of Rattlesnake Mountain that stood to the south. We climbed that mountain many times and I was always fascinated by the simple wooden cross, painted white and planted in a rock at the top. Nana and Papa were active in Emmanuel Episcopal Church, the church that Nana's mother, Sadie Gwin Harris, had helped establish when San Angelo was new and near the edge of the frontier of an expanding nation. My mother always referred to my great grandmother, Sadie Gwin Harris, as Gran. Miss Sadie Gwin had been a young woman from Georgia when she went to turn-of-the-century San Angelo, a hub of West Texas ranching, to marry Ralph Harris, my great grandfather. Born in 1874, Gran witnessed the coming of the automobile, telephones and both World Wars before she had a stroke in her sixties or seventies. She then lived for years - maybe 12 or so - in that nether-world, cared for by kindly nurses in a quiet wing of the local hospital. Or so I imagine it. She was already there in January, 1955. I assume that Gran never knew how her daughter, Helen, was killed.

The Harris family wealth was generated in West Texas over four generations that grew from roots in Texas when it was still a Mexican territory. I only knew Gran through the stories mother told and the photos on the wall. I came to understand more about her from a tattered copy of a newspaper article about the 20th Century Club, a social organization that she joined in its infancy and helped support throughout her life, forming deep friendships through the sharing of life's joys and tragedies with other women along the way. That Club grew into an elite group of women of means. It is easy to label these women as entitled socialites. But I see Gran now as simply a young woman in a dusty cow town on the Texas prairie, doing her best to find enjoyment in a routine life. In 1903, her first child, my Nana, Helen, was born. Then came three others – Ralph Jr, Gwin and Ledyard. Gran devoted her time to raising her children, supporting the growth of Emmanuel Episcopal Church and reaching out with her friendliness to other women in her social circles – and perhaps beyond. In this way, she helped to water the tender young roots of the Anglo-European way of life that was taking hold in the plains where this continent's first peoples had roamed for centuries.

The area evolved. Gran's children grew. She became a woman of privilege, thanks to the success of the ranching and then – in an even bigger way – when oil was discovered underneath all those acres in May of 1923. It was around that time that she and Ralph built a large and stately home on the corner of Beauregard and Koenigheim in the heart of the town.

Gran's daughter, Helen (my Nana), dodged the bullet of the alcoholism that ran through the family line. Nana's little brother, Ledyard, the fourth born, was not so lucky. With ambitions other than ranching, Ledyard got a start in a professional career but succumbed quickly to the pull of the drink and became destitute. Nana sent him money every day. Not too much. Just enough to keep him comfortable but not so much that he would get rolled and robbed once he drank himself into a stupor. In return for this kindness, Nana inherited her little brother's share of the family land. This was contested in court; the case was found in favor of Nana. My mother told me that the court ruling left a residue of tension among Nana and some of her siblings.

After she married Hicks Allen, Nana gave birth to her own children in the hospital across the street from her parents' home. After her divorce, she had trained to become a teacher but married Harry Weaver before she began to work. Harry Weaver, the well-to-do architect from Houston, then became "Papa" to my aunt, Sadie Gwin Allen, and my mother, Helen Allen.

My ancestors were pioneers, descended from European immigrants – Scotch, Irish, English. I imagine them as adventurous souls, living on the edge of America at the turn of the 20th Century. Nana loved the land and taught her daughters to love it as well. She continued the family tradition of ranching and became a well-respected cattlewoman herself – not an easy feat for a woman in that era, that location and that livelihood. Although the region has dried up a little bit every year since then, at the time it was relatively lush prairie land southeast of Abilene, Texas. Long low mountains with mostly flat tops make the area look like iconic Texas – big skies, expansive views and sparse vegetation – like the country so typical of a John Ford western.

Nana and Papa looked after Gran's house in town and occasionally stayed there overnight or for a few days before returning to the ranch. In 1955, on Tuesday, January 18th, they arrived in San Angelo from a trip to Houston. Papa still had business interests in Houston - rental property and perhaps other things. Nana must have enjoyed a visit with her older daughter. My three cousins were all born by then and would have been toddlers to school-aged – probably a true delight for their grandmother.

My aunt followed in her mother's footsteps and excelled academically. My mother did not. Even though she was very intelligent, Helen just couldn't be bothered with higher education. She didn't find a career either, which would have been nearly impossible in those times anyway. It seems that young women - and especially young women from privileged families - were just expected to meet and marry someone and then set about having families of their own. I recall stories my mother told about wanting to become an actress. Of course her family would not hear of it. My mother definitely had a rebellious streak in her. She was popular through high school but she was constantly bothered by her mother's frustration with her poor grades. So my mother buckled down one semester and got all A's. She brought home the report card and told her mother, "There! I've done it! And don't ever expect me to do it again!" She had the brains but, apparently, not the ambition. After graduation from high school she enrolled at the University of Texas in Austin. She pledged a sorority which she told me was of her mother's choosing, not her own. While she may have enjoyed the social life, she didn't continue for long at The University - probably only one semester.

She returned to live at her parents' home, then still in Houston. She showed no signs of snagging a husband and settling into her own family life. Entering into a marriage was such an integral part of a young woman's life in that day that Nana and Papa probably felt it was their duty to help Helen find a suitable mate. Papa introduced my mother to her first husband. The man's photography studio was located in the same building as the architectural firm where Papa was working at the time. Aunt Sadie Gwin told me that everyone in the family was aware that the man came from the "wrong side of the tracks" but that they graciously accepted him anyway. Mother later told us that she was forced to marry the man and never really wanted to. My father told me that mother was aware that Papa and Nana wanted to enjoy the freedom of retirement by travelling and felt they could not do that as long as they had an unmarried daughter at home. The wedding portrait that hangs on my wall certainly bears witness to my mother's reluctance - a beautiful young woman in a stunning satin gown with flowers all around, but no joy in the eyes of the bride and a resolute expression on her face. There is a severity to her stiffness, certain darkness to her demeanor.

On that trip to Houston in January, 1955, Papa (Mr. Weaver) had his toolbox with him when he visited several of his rental properties with the intent of repairing any minor problems. He may also have gone into a storage shed on one of the properties. He'd had lunch with a realtor and discussed the profitability of buying more rental property in the area. The Houston paper detailed Papa's every move that day because my Nana was murdered the day after.

On Wednesday, January 19th, Nana and Papa woke up at Gran's house on Beauregard Street in San Angelo, having driven in from Houston the day before. The drive from San Angelo to Houston is about 375 miles and currently takes about 6 hours. In 1955, it must have taken longer. The cars were bigger, maybe slower and probably took a lot more effort to drive. So, I imagine they were both quite tired the night they returned. The local paper[1] reported that they ate out Tuesday evening and retired early. It appears that they left the Chevrolet they'd taken to Houston parked in the driveway overnight, perhaps partially blocking the other Chevrolet in the driveway. Nana got up the next morning and prepared to go visit her mother (my Gran) in the hospital. Papa would have gone with her as he usually did for such visits but, on that day, Nana had an appointment at the beauty shop later and then was due to sit in for Gran at the monthly meeting of the 20th Century Club. So Papa had planned to stay at Gran's house until Nana returned.

The folks at the gas station across the street from Gran's house told reporters what they had seen around the cars that morning. Nana's exit from the house, the driveway and the two Chevrolets were all visible from across Koenigheim Street to the east. The station owner, Mr. Lamb, his wife and a station attendant by the name of John Ramirez said they saw Mr. Harry Weaver go out to the car and remove some papers from the glove box. Mr. Lamb later said that watching the scene made him think it was about time to service the Weavers' car again. The three of them found nothing unusual about Mr. Weaver's behavior because they had seen him repeat a similar routine at other times when his wife was going to take that car. The local paper does not mention that Mr. Weaver opened the trunk of the other Chevrolet in the driveway and left it open. The Lambs *are* quoted as telling law enforcement officials that they did not see Mr. Weaver open the *hood* of any car that morning. About a week later, the Houston Post summed up what Mr. Weaver told them about his activities that morning "... he walked out of the house to get some carpenter tools from the car used on the Houston trip and put them in the car he uses on trips to the ranch. He had taken the tools to

Houston to repair some rental property. He took the tools from his wife's car, he said, and put them in the one he calls the ranch car. As he closed the trunk of the ranch car, he noticed that the key ring for the keys he had used to open his wife's car was broken. He hammered the key ring back together then put the ignition key into the switch of his wife's car. Then he slammed the door of that car and walked back into the house."[2]

According to the local San Angelo paper, the service station folks said that about half an hour later, Mrs. Harry E. Weaver stepped out the back door "wearing a red coat and carrying a purse with a long strap." Mr. Lamb added, "She got in and sat down in the car and, as far as I know, before she shut the car door, it exploded."[3]

The local paper recounts, "Apparently touched off by nitroglycerin, the blast was heard by thousands of San Angeloans in the downtown area."[4] A car salesman by the name of Clinton Behrens, of Charles Motor Company, Used Car Lot, testified at the Grand Jury that he had heard the explosion and saw, "everything go up."[5] Mr. Lamb called police right away and then ran across the street. He later said, "She was inside, slumping over and gasping."[6] A doctor who was next door to the service station, Dr. R.E. Capshaw, also heard the explosion and went to the scene. Mr. Weaver had come out, gone back in and, at the time the doctor was arriving, had returned with a sheet, which he placed over his wife's head and torso. The doctor is quoted as saying, "Mr. Weaver was more or less in a state of shock."[7] I wonder whether Papa went in to get the sheet in order to protect the dignity of his beloved or was the scene simply too horrific to do anything but shield it from view. Both, I imagine.

An ambulance took my grandmother to Shannon Hospital where she died a few minutes later at 8:55 am on Wednesday, January 19th, 1955. She was 51 years and about three months old.

It is interesting to look at old newspapers - a little slice of life in that period of time. The San Angelo Standard Times was in its 27th year in 1955 and boasted "Exclusive West Texas News for West Texans."[8] That day's issue had 24 pages. I was able to talk by phone with the reporter/photographer who covered most of the story for the Standard Times. Joe North said he had been sent out on that Wednesday morning to City Hall to take photographs of some of the local politicians who were due at an early morning meeting. The required quorum of people was not present and the meeting never came to order. Mr. North took no photos there and instead returned to the newspaper office with his 4X5 camera loaded with film. His editor said nothing was going on. Then Mr. North felt the vibration of the explosion and said, "Something's going on now!" He ran the three blocks to the Harris home where my grandmother's injured body had already been taken by the ambulance. He took pictures and interviewed those present. He also said he encouraged Texas Ranger, Ralph Rohatsch to go to Houston to interview a businessman who had been mentioned by Mr. Weaver as a likely suspect. Mr. North told me he was later scolded by the Ranger for leading him on a wild goose chase, since the lead had not panned out.[9]

The next day's local headline read, "Rangers Grill Houston Man in Fatal Angelo Car Blast." The man was not named. Instead he is described as "A 38-year-old businessman." He was questioned for two hours by four Texas Rangers and then put in a car with his two children and returned to his home in a well-to-do area in Houston. Apparently reporters tried and failed to get additional information from the man himself. The Rangers and San Angelo Sheriff, Cecil Turner, did mention that the 38-year-old businessman "hasn't been forgotten."[10] The Houston Post later reported that this man had refused to take a lie detector test. [11]

The shock of the explosion reverberated in the newspaper stories for days. Almost all of the front page on Thursday, January 20th was devoted to the explosion and death of my grandmother. A photo of the "death scene" showed a rope designating the area of the investigation. Onlookers were lined up all along it. Mr. Lamb, the service station owner, estimated that by the end of the day about a thousand people had been by to look at the scene. He also said that, after the explosion, he found the car's windshield wiper in the driveway of his service station. Additional debris was reportedly scattered over a "wide area." By mid-afternoon, the police were inspecting the other cars for explosive devices.[12]

In Houston on that day, the headline read, "Houston 'Lead' Fails in Car Bomb Death Probe".[13] The article described the Rangers' investigation into the 38 year-old businessman. The San Angelo paper reported that the Tom Green County Justice of the Peace, J. P. Holberg, was "withholding verdict on Mrs. Weaver's death pending further investigation by city police and sheriff's department."[14] The local paper also carried the announcement of arrangements for her burial on the next day, Friday, at Emmanuel Episcopal Church with Reverend Morris Elliott officiating and the burial afterward at Fairmount Cemetery. Reverend Elliott was still the priest when I went to church at Emmanuel Episcopal as a child. A round-faced and very loving man, I remember him most vividly bending down to shake my tiny hand in the doorway of the church following the service. His soft gaze seemed to reach down deep within me. I knew that he knew my mother well. He was an occasional guest at our ranch and had a keen interest in archaeology. I seem to remember that he had an impressive collection of arrowheads, but I never saw them. Years later, in 1981, he buried my mother as well with an appropriate balance of soothing professionalism and just enough emotion in his voice to honor the friendship they had built over the years.

A tone of shock and dismay runs through the accounts of this unbelievable crime. I perceive an undercurrent of respect for the family that is both heartening and surprising, but I may be imagining it. The Weavers were apparently quite good friends of Mr. Houston Harte, who published the San Angelo Standard Times. Just eight years after the explosion, my parents moved us into a home they built down the street from the Hartes. I don't recall him at all and I only saw his wife in their kitchen window. My dearest childhood friend and I had permission to cut through their yard to visit each other's houses. I would like to think that my family members were grateful for the respect and sensitivity with which the story was reported locally. But I am not sure any reporting would have been seen in a positive light at the time, especially since the early search for a suspect seemed to go no further than my Papa, Mr. Weaver.

That first day after the explosion, a crowd of investigative professionals descended on the scene. Individuals from the Texas Department of Public Safety (DPS) in Austin arrived in a private plane piloted by the fingerprint expert, Mr. Jack Mercer. Mr. J.D. Chastain was the chemist and Mr. George Burney was the Texas Ranger demolitions expert. They reportedly "had no doubts" on the afternoon of the 20th about the actual cause of my Grandmother's demise. "A bomb, possibly composed of nitroglycerin, was discharged near the left side of the engine block." It had been planted "beside the engine block, on the left side about midway between the engine's top and the steering gear."[15] These were the sturdy and spacious automobiles of the 1950s – lots of room in the engine compartment and very little concern about excess weight, since gasoline was so cheap that no one worried about conserving it.

The article describes the wreckage but erroneously refers to a *truck* when what is meant is that the *trunk* of the Chevrolet was not destroyed by the blast. "The radiator was blasted forward and barely was secured to the car's frame on the right side. And the vehicle's dashboard was pushed backward almost to the back of the front seat. ... Parts of the demolished automobile's intake manifold were found inside the trunk of the Chevrolet parked near the death car. ... Weaver told authorities he, himself, had left the truck [*sic*] open after transferring some articles from one car to the other early Wednesday before the explosion. ... Examination of the Cadillac and Buick, which were inside the double garage, was deferred until it was determined the second Chevrolet contained no bomb. ... The Cadillac, the car Mrs. Weaver ordinarily used, was next to be checked. ... After Burney traced all live wires and all places bombs are known to have been planted, Detective Sgt. Lee Braziel of the San Angelo Police Department started the car and backed it into the driveway beside the two Chevrolets. By early evening, the experts had determined to their satisfaction that the one remaining vehicle, the Buick, had not been tampered with either. Chastain said examination of the wreckage revealed no definite means by which the bomb was detonated. Earlier, local police had located a small strand of copper wire on the ignition switch and speculated it may have given the bomb its igniting spark." Chastain is credited with determining the explosion to have been caused by nitroglycerin because of the "stench of the explosive which was still heavy about the debris."[16]

Below the fold on the front page is a photo of three men in the back yard of the Beauregard residence. Mr. Weaver has mostly his back to the camera. Capt. Ray Butler and George Burney, the DPS demolition man are seen in the picture. Mr. Weaver is in his shirtsleeves and the other two are wearing lightweight jackets. The winter sun can get very warm in West Texas.

Several photos complete the picture of the horrific scene. A shot of the driver's area of the car shows the steering wheel, once round, looking like two semicircles joined at their bases with a ninety-degree angle between them instead of the smooth 180 degrees of the original flat wheel. The wheel was bent in half by the force of the blast! The door is gone; it was presumably blown off. The caption reads, in part, "Note the shoe wrested from her foot."[17] The explosion blew her out of her shoes. Of course it would have. What a bizarre thing - to be instantly removed from items over which one normally has had complete control. The shoes she walked in as she approached the car to drive to several appointments during what would otherwise have been a very ordinary day. A view of the yard indicates the path that my grandmother took from the door of her mother's house to the car parked outside a freestanding garage. Two naked trees looked unperturbed in the winter sunshine spilling into the yard and the open area beyond it.

Still another photo shows the scene from what appears to be a second story angle. I can't really imagine reporters getting permission to enter the home to take the photo, but the angle does suggest strangers walking up the staircase, wandering down the hall to find a window for a full overview of the scene. The car's engine compartment is shattered; both fenders gone. One fender may be lying next to the car. As I examined this photo I began to get a sense of the invasion of privacy that my mother alluded to emotionally throughout her life as she struggled to resolve her grief over her mother's tragic death.

The reporting was effective though; the enormous destructive force of the blast is absolutely clear. The photographer, Joe North, told me that there was so much interest in the story that Houston Harte established a temporary office in New York in order to make the photos of the event accessible. That strikes me as within the bounds of ethical journalism. I don't know how my family felt about that at that time or if they were even aware of it. I guess it's just as true now as it was then that many decent humans are simply fascinated by the horror which those among us are capable of perpetrating on others.

The implications for my grandmother were overwhelmingly disturbing when I first read the account and saw the pictures. That she survived for even a few minutes is unbelievable. After some time sitting with this information, looking at the pictures and grasping the shock and savagery of the crime, I calmed myself with my own belief that the essence of who she was had already embarked on her journey Home even as her body remained on the seat of that car, gasping for breath.

CHAPTER TWO

Arrest

It's better to burn than to disappear.
~Albert Camus

The investigation began immediately, of course. Newspaper accounts were delayed by one day, owing to the fact that the information of the day travelled at the pace of telephone reporting with an actual human creating typesetting, perhaps letter by letter. So every newspaper reported the previous day's events - a warp in time which seems archaic compared to our current age of instantaneous news.

The first order of business was to establish the safety and integrity of the crime scene. Then came the pursuit of the question - how did the blast occur and why? That first day after the explosion, the local paper shows a San Angelo policeman pointing to the "Lethal Gadget."[18] The ignition switch, in what remained of the engine of the car, dangled by a single strand of wire from the "demolished dashboard."[19] Automatic switches were the most prevalent means of igniting such an explosion so that was the presumed method of detonation. It appeared that all of the evidence had been destroyed by the blast itself.

The paper that day also included news about the Weavers, their wealth and lifestyle, beneath the headline, "Hospitality Famed At Weaver Ranch."[20] A photograph shows a gathering for Easter in 1954 – the previous spring – at their ranch in Coke County. They hosted the Easter Sunday Sunrise Service for the entire congregation of Emmanuel Episcopal Church each year. Everyone was invited to stay for breakfast and "hundreds" were said to have attended. The Ralph Harris Family "was among the organizers" of the Emmanuel Episcopal Church of San Angelo.[21] All of this must have had something to do with the captivating cross on top of Rattlesnake Mountain. My father tells me that, years later, someone visiting the ranch asked if that cross had something to do with "that lady that died."

The eulogy for Helen Harris Weaver, which was part of the same article, reveals more than I ever knew about my grandmother – the facts of her life and the shades of her personality. It describes Nana as "… a competent ranch woman. She knew grasses and their protein content and was able to guess livestock weights within a few pounds simply by looking at the animals. … [she was] … of medium stature … blonde with animated blue eyes. Her direct gaze was analytical and productive of logical comments on any subject. A low-pitched voice which carried well was a compliment to her choice of words and her vocabulary which reflected years of study. In 1921 she was graduated from San Angelo High School as valedictorian of her class. School records at that time lauded Miss Helen Harris and noted that she had been offered a scholarship to any of the leading universities in the state for her scholastic attainment."[22] The paper described her as "a brilliant student,"[23] and then related that Nana had received a scholarship medal while in the West Ward School. Apparently, Mrs. Will Viney, a former schoolteacher, presented my grandmother with a gold medal which Mrs. Viney herself had received in earlier years. Inscribed on the medal was the word, "Perfect." Mrs. Viney had added my grandmother's name, "Helen" to the inscription. The medal honored the fact that she had not missed a single day of school from first grade through twelfth.

Nana attended the University of Texas, married before graduating, had her two daughters and then divorced. She later obtained her advanced degree at Incarnate Word College in San Antonio and planned to teach school. She married Harry Weaver instead, in San Antonio in 1936. They moved to Houston and then, when Weaver went into partial retirement some years later, they relocated to the property in Coke County, north of San Angelo. The article concludes by saying, "Her main activities outside of her home were centered around church, work and the local Planned Parenthood Board of which she was president in 1952."[24]

On Friday, the investigation continued as the local headline read, "Bomb Hunt Fails At Weaver Ranch."[25] The team of experts from Austin, along with the local investigator, Detective Sgt. Lee Braziel and the Tom Green County Sheriff, Cecil Turner, was involved in the search of the Weaver's Ranch house just off highway 305 - the road from San Angelo to the tiny town of Robert Lee and other points north. The Weavers had not been at the ranch house for almost a week prior to the explosion.

The Grand Jury, which had been in session when the explosion took place was recessed subject to call-back. Meanwhile Justice of the Peace J.B. Holberg waited for more information, including a final doctor's report and the results of a chemical analysis of specimens sent to Austin, before initiating an inquest verdict. San Angelo Chief of Police, Clarence Lowe, said he had been speaking with a longtime friend of the Weavers, Mr. Mart Findlater, to investigate who may have had a motive to plant the bomb. Mr. Lowe also talked with Mr. Ralph Harris, Jr. (my great uncle) of Uvalde. Ranger Rohatsch reportedly said the 38-year-old businessman from Houston had not been dropped as a suspect.[26]

The Houston Post newspaper on Friday, January 21st states that Mr. Weaver reported to police that he might have seen the businessman in a store in Houston. The so-called Death Car was the same one the couple used to drive to Houston. So, for a time, authorities were wondering whether the bomb was placed in the car during the couple's stay in Houston. The Post says, "The man had previously threatened the family, and it was theorized that if the man suddenly discovered that the San Angelo family were in Houston, an old urge to carry out the threat might have overtaken him. ... But ... officers now believe the death bomb was not a time bomb." They deduced this logically. "... the killer would have no certainty that his victim would be in the car at the time he picked for the explosion. ... a time bomb usually cannot be set to explode more than 12 hours away from the time it is primed. The mechanism work [sic] like a clock and completes a cycle in 12 hours. The explosion was touched off about 24 hours after the Weavers left Houston. If this is correct, the Houston man isn't implicated unless he went to San Angelo or unless he had an accomplice. Although all sources were close-mouthed about the Houston end of the investigation, it is known that the 38 year-old man as well as his children reported the man was in Houston both Tuesday and Wednesday. Presumably the investigators have no information to contradict this claim."[27] The Post then offers this about the car, "The Death Car was used primarily as a ranch car, Sheriff Turner said. Although it was regularly used by both Mr. and Mrs. Weaver, the wife used it more than the husband."[28]

The funeral took place as planned at 2:00 pm on Friday, January 21st, as a curious twist in the case began to play out. The local headline on Sunday read, "Call Seeks Cash For Bomb Killer."[29] Apparently, someone had telephoned Papa at the home on Beauregard Avenue and told him to send $3,000. to Ardmore, Oklahoma in order to obtain a picture of his wife's killer.

Papa got the call at about 3:30 pm on Friday, January 21st. The paper reports that the home had been guarded by a policeman every night since the bomb exploded. "Weaver was instructed to send the money to General Delivery, Ardmore, if possible before Monday."[30] Papa apparently tried to stall the man by saying he did not have the cash on hand but that he would send it as soon as he could get it. Then he informed local police of the call. Apparently the Ardmore police were notified and were watching the post office on Saturday until it closed at noon. The surveillance was called off after a paper in Houston got wind of the call and published the whole story.

On Saturday, authorities had convened the Grand Jury and had heard testimony from Mr. Weaver and several others. An article in the local paper that morning gave details of this headline, "Estate Left To Husband, Daughters."[31] It was public information at that point that my mother, my aunt and Papa all stood to benefit financially from the tragic death of their loved one. I can't imagine a situation of greater ambivalence and emotional conflict.

A Monday Standard Times headline read "Progress Reported in Bombing Death."[32] In San Angelo, District Attorney, Aubrey B. Stokes, had said the night before that "strong evidence"[33] had emerged in the case. He declined to give details but alluded to "… a great deal of progress in the case in the last few days."[34] He would not name suspects.

Curiously, Papa's son, Earl, (from a previous marriage) had been seen quickly leaving the house on Beauregard at about 9 a.m. on Sunday morning, the 23rd. He reportedly used the phone at the service station across the street to call the police. He told police that he was afraid the house might be blown up and that he was fearful of staying in the home. The chief of police, Clarence Lowe, was told of the call and arrived at the home a few minutes later when a search took place. No cause for concern was discovered and Mr. Earl Weaver was given a ride to the airport where he caught a plane back to Houston.

It is not clear what spooked Harry Weaver's son that Sunday but I wonder if his father related to him the story of the night a few years prior to the murder, when Harry Weaver and my grandmother were held at gunpoint in their home at the Coke County ranch. A man demanded money and threatened to kill Mr. Weaver if he didn't get it. He instructed my grandmother to write a suicide note, seemingly written by her husband, saying that he had been implicated in Senator McCarthy's hunt for communists and chose to kill himself instead of facing the charges. My father tells me that Nana wrote the note as instructed but made lots of grammatical and spelling errors so that anyone reading it would have known that Mr. Weaver did not actually write it. I had assumed that the couple paid the man and he went away, since they lived to tell the story. But the Houston Post reported that Mr. Weaver actually talked the man out of his threats. Apparently no money changed hands that night but one of the newspaper articles made reference to a Coke County civil matter that was dropped by the Weavers against the man sometime after that evening, before my grandmother's murder. The Houston Post identifies this man as the mysterious 38 year-old businessman from Houston and adds that, "The sheriff said he knows of no one other than the Houston man who has threatened the wealthy couple." [35]

The investigative team - District Attorney Stokes, Sheriff Cecil Turner and Ranger Ralph Rohatsch - reportedly met to discuss "a new angle in the case, likely to develop Monday."[36] Then on Tuesday, the local headline read, "Bomb Death Case Reaches Standstill."[37] The D.A. was out of town and had let folks know he was following up on a lead that emerged the day before. But, as of 11 p.m. Monday night, January 24th, the San Angelo Standard Times had no new news to report in the case.

On Wednesday the 26th, The Houston Post had plenty to report regarding the interview in San Angelo with Mr. Weaver and his attorney. The standstill in the case seemed to reflect a standoff that had been brewing between the D.A. and the recently bereaved Mr. Weaver. It appears that the San Angelo authorities, with D.A. Stokes in the lead, were convinced that Mr. Weaver killed his wife. He was, after all, seen in and around the automobiles just before the lethal explosion. He certainly had a lot to gain financially, according to Helen Weaver's will - various properties and assets as well as the right to occupy the Coke County home he had built for them. But this was also a man who had created his own wealth; a man who was observed by a medical doctor to be in a state of shock as he tended to his dying wife in the wreckage of their car.

Yet Papa also had developed a friendship with a local woman, a divorcee, by the name of Helen Adams. She was among the few people who were called to testify at the initial Grand Jury inquiry on Saturday, January 23rd. She had no idea why she had been called and she told reporters she had no information about the case. The early focus on her suggests that D.A. Stokes was indeed trying to make a case for Papa as the murderer with his possible romantic involvement with Mrs. Adams as motive. She recounted that she had known Mr. Weaver for many years, having made his acquaintance when she owned a record store where he shopped. She had closed the shop and subsequently opened Helen's Lounge in the same location. She said she had remained friends with both Mr. and Mrs. Weaver and testified that Mr. Weaver had never taken a drink at her pub in all the years she ran it.

On Thursday, January 27th, the Post reported that Mrs. Adams had a concern that her own life might be in danger. She was aware that she had become associated with the crime by virtue of her Grand Jury testimony. She stated to reporters, "I cringe every time I start my car."[38]

The Post had reported on Monday, the 24th, that D.A. Aubrey Stokes was thinking an arrest was imminent and that the perpetrator, "... very likely is walking around on San Angelo streets at this time."[39] Also that day, Mr. Stokes told reporters, "We stumbled onto something good."[40] He then refused to elaborate except to say that he believed the suspect "knows we're after him."[41]

Mr. Weaver's attorney, Mr. Carl Runge, responded to that by talking with the press about his dismay at the number of rumors floating around town. He said, "What happens ... is that people are getting third- and fourth-hand information. ... I've been practicing law for nearly 40 years and I've never heard such nonsense before. ... Instead of finding out facts about the case ... and then arresting the man, they've picked out the man they want to try and now they're trying to find something that will enable them to bring him to trial."[42] Mr. Runge pointed out that Mr. Weaver had offered to take a lie detector test and only withdrew that offer on the advice of his attorneys. Mr. Weaver told Houston Post reporters, "I was very much in love with my wife - now as much as ever in our 15 or 16 years of marriage. That's about all I can say - except that I didn't kill her."[43] It was later in this interview that Mr. Weaver explained his actions around the cars the morning of his wife's death: opening a trunk, getting out tools and repairing a key ring. After he put the key in the ignition for my Grandmother, he slammed the car door and went back inside.

This explanation of his actions telegraphs why so much attention was focused on Mr. Weaver. It would be suspicious if he had actually been stupid enough to set up an explosion in daylight and in full view of people across the street. His attorney, Mr. Runge commented, "If Mr. Weaver had known that the car was wired to blow up, he wouldn't have risked slamming the door."[44] The article goes on to say that Mr. Runge thought the investigation was being carelessly handled and that officers had been very slow in getting in touch with the Houston man; so slow that, Mr. Runge asserted, a Houston reporter talked with the Houston man before the authorities did. Mr. Runge also pointed out his great dismay that information regarding the telephone call from the Ardmore, Oklahoma man was given to the newspapers prematurely causing that initial investigation to fail.

On Wednesday the 26th, the San Angelo Standard Times reported that the guards, who had been posted day and night at the Harris home on Beauregard where Mr. Weaver was staying, had been "removed" as of Tuesday night. That seems to be an interesting response to the criticism of the local authorities' handling of the case. But it could also, of course, be mere coincidence. The paper adds that police had been patrolling past the residence frequently during the preceding nights since the explosion.

On Thursday morning, the local headline announced, "Weaver Says His Life May Be In Danger."[45] Papa let it be known that he believed the bomb might have been meant for him, too. "I many times left with Mrs. Weaver to go to the hospital and there are people that know I went. ... It was natural for me to go with her to the hospital that day. I hadn't gone in four, five or six days."[46] It was Mrs. Weaver's later appointment at a beauty shop and plans to attend a meeting that caused Mr. Weaver to decline to join his wife that morning. Mr. Weaver had been interviewed the day before, on Wednesday, in the presence of his attorney. Mr. Weaver opened the interview saying, "I want to look a man in the eye. I have nothing to hide."[47] He ended the interview saying, "Something will happen some place because nobody has gotten away with anything like this."[48] The article then points out that, "While talking to newsmen, Weaver frequently referred to his late wife as 'Mommy'."[49]

With little new information emerging and with local authorities seeming to focus only on Mr. Weaver, the family decided to offer a reward. They arranged it through Mr. Runge, who announced it to the press late on Wednesday, January 26th. The reward for information leading to the arrest of the person responsible for the murder specified that such information be given to Mr. Weaver directly.

To say that District Attorney Stokes was not a fan of that approach definitely understates the situation. He took exception to the offer because it cut his office out of access to any information generated by the reward. But the arrangements ensured that Mr. Weaver and the family would obtain any critical information; it guaranteed that such information would not be inadvertently leaked to the press.

The skirmish that this ignited was also reported in Thursday morning's local paper. It seemed that District Attorney Stokes and local law enforcement were not looking much farther than the victim's family home on Beauregard for a suspect. Mr. Weaver grew weary of being in their sights while the perpetrator remained free and continued to pose a potential threat to him personally. The local paper published Mr. Runge's statement in full for the interest of local readers: "The family of Mr. and Mrs. Harry E. Weaver of San Angelo, Tex., offers a reward of $10,000.00 for information leading to the arrest and final conviction of the person or persons responsible for her death by bombing on Jan. 19, 1955."[50]

District Attorney Stokes responded by announcing to the press his displeasure at the way the reward had been offered. He said, "I feel that the offer is worthless to the State of Texas as it now stands. And I represent the State of Texas. As the offer now stands, it does in no way help or aid in the prosecution of this case. But, on the contrary, it will hinder the prosecution of the real murderer and tend to defeat justice. ... I also feel that if this offer is made in good faith, the money should be put in escrow and paid on the condition that the information be sent directly to the district attorney's office. ... For, in every criminal case, information should be sent to the prosecuting attorney. The district attorney is responsible for the prosecution of this case. I respectfully request that all evidence pertaining to this be delivered personally to my office. Anyone having evidence in the case may contact me day or night. Information or evidence that would lead to the final conviction in this case might be lost forever unless given directly to the district attorney's office."[51]

When asked to respond to the D.A.'s message, Carl Runge simply said, "No comment."[52]

My father told me that the investigation had bogged down so much, the family, on advice of Mr. Runge, offered the reward. The initial debate was whether the amount would be $5,000. or $10,000. - quite a lot of money in 1955. A new, three bedroom home, not far away in Amarillo, went for $12,000. in that era.

Bob Rohatsch, the son of Ranger Rohatsch, recalled that his father was genuinely perplexed by the case. He spoke with me by phone and let me know that his father died in 1974, suddenly, of a stroke as he ate his lunch. He is remembered in the Texas Rangers Hall of Fame in Waco, Texas. Texas Rangers were unique lawmen in many ways, one of which is that they were allowed to possess their own copies of case files. Some of those case files have ended up in the museum in Waco, but not Mr. Rohatsch's, or so I was told by phone when I called the Rangers' Hall of Fame.

After the posting of the reward offer, the local paper reported little in the way of fresh news about the case for several days. That could have been because the investigation shifted back to Houston. According to the Post, on Thursday evening the 27th of January, Mr. Stokes and Ranger Rohatsch arrived in Houston at about 7:15 p.m. but "remained silent as sphinxes about the Weaver case."[53] Post reporters apparently informed Mr. Stokes of Mr. Weaver's shed on the rental property and, at that time, Mr. Stokes indicated he would be looking into it. If that is accurate, it suggests to me that Mr. Stokes, at that time, still held that Mr. Weaver was the murderer. But there was a Houston angle which provided a very different perspective on the case. When Mr. Stokes was asked more directly why he had come to Houston, he deferred to Rohatsch who said, "It wouldn't be smart to say what we came here for before we do it."[54]

The article continues, recounting that another Texas Ranger from Houston took the two of them out for dinner. They returned to the Sheriff's office at about 9:20, chatted with Houston deputies for about an hour and then conferred in a private office until about midnight. Just after midnight, very early on Friday, January 28th, Stokes and Rohatsch left the Sheriff's Department and told reporters they were going to "get some sleep."[55]

The article goes on to identify Mr. Weaver's rental property on 705 Drew Avenue and to give details of Mr. Weaver's visit to the property in the days prior to his wife's murder. Some tenants and neighbors gave interviews to reporters who wrote, "Mrs. Brimble and other old friends around the neighborhood expressed puzzlement at Mr. Weaver being considered a suspect by anyone in his wife's murder. All voiced belief in his innocence."[56] Someone else is quoted as saying, "I think the bomb must have been meant for him, not his wife. ... when you go up in the world you are bound to step on some toes along the way."[57] The photocopy from the microfiche of the paper is very hard to read here, so the quote may not be entirely accurate and the name of the speaker is illegible.

Another article in the Post that day relates the springing of a second trap in Ardmore, Oklahoma. The phone caller who had requested $3,000. in return for a photo of the killer apparently called back after learning that Weaver had gone to the authorities with news of the first call. He said to Mr. Weaver, "You double-crossed me. Send that money and don't double-cross me again, or I'll get you."[58] Mr. Weaver sent $500. and a note inviting the man to earn $9,500. more by providing information, referring, of course, to the reward. The letter was mailed to General Delivery to Kelly Rose, as instructed. Weaver sent the envelope with the requirement for a signature by the person picking it up.

This time Ardmore detectives were waiting when a 14 year-old boy claimed the letter. John Dellano Staffano, a reformatory escapee, was followed down the street then arrested at around 9 a.m. on Thursday. He eventually led police to Jack Ray Cordell, age 32, previously of Brownwood, Texas. Cordell allowed himself to be extradited back to Texas without realizing that they were returning him to Brownwood first to face an outstanding swindling charge. He was interviewed in Stephenville, Texas by representatives of San Angelo law enforcement. From Houston, when D.A. Stokes was discussing this development of the case he said, "I believe that guy is just a confidence man looking for some easy money. I don't think he has any valuable information about the case."[59]

Reporting on the Friday developments in the case, Saturday's Post headline read, "Weaver Not Top Suspect, D.A. Says After Houston Sleuthing."[60] District Attorney Stokes is reported to have no change in his theory of the case after spending all of Friday in Houston, "picking up bits of evidence." He stated, "I still feel about the same as I did before I got here." When reporters learned that Stokes would not be seeking a search warrant to examine Weaver's locked shed in Houston, there were questions about how the D.A. was going about pursuing his number one suspect. The D.A. responded with this quip, "Weaver named himself as the Number 1 suspect. We consider him a suspect - not as the Number 1."[61]

The Houston newspaper reports had generated a lot of citizen interest in the shed on Drew Street. "Large numbers"[62] of automobiles were reported driving by the place in the 700 block of Drew during the evening. The Weavers had lived in that house on Drew Street as newlyweds.

On Sunday, January 30th, the news of the arrest of my grandmother's killer was emblazoned on the front page of the Post: "Forgotten Man, Ex-In-Law, Charged in Car-Bomb Death."[63] District Attorney Stokes had been in Houston since Thursday. On Friday evening around 7 p.m., he was in his Texas State Hotel room when Houston Police Chief Heard called him. Several hours later, at around 2 a.m. on Saturday, January 29th, the Houston authorities accompanied

District Attorney Stokes and Ranger Rohatsch to the home of Harry Leonard Washburn to arrest him. The Local paper recounted that Ranger Rohatsch, "armed with the telegraphic warrant from San Angelo Justice J.B. Holberg, knocked on the downstairs door. After a while Washburn, in pajamas, came to an upstairs porch and asked who it was. ... Washburn was very calm."[64] He opened the door, got dressed and made arrangements with his neighbors to care for the two children. He was arrested at 3 a.m.

Washburn, my mother's first husband, was the "38 year-old businessman" who had already been questioned by law enforcement but not named and not even mentioned much in the papers since his initial interrogation. The papers did say he had not been forgotten in the investigation. Washburn told a Houston Post reporter that he sort of liked Mrs. Weaver and that if he were going to harm anyone it would have been Mr. Weaver for whom he stated he held an "intense dislike." He said that he had long ago decided to "... let bygones be bygones. ... I wouldn't want to kill her. Why, only last summer, I got an anonymous letter in the mail from San Angelo. It contained five $100 bills for my two children. I'm pretty sure from the handwriting that it was from Mrs. Weaver, their grandmother. If I had still wanted to kill a Weaver, it would have been Harry and not Helen."[65]

Still? Did he really say "still wanted to kill"? The Post printed it. I suppose that even Washburn was not denying that he had threatened to kill them at the Coke County ranch in 1951.

Washburn repeated his previously given alibi information, stating at the time of the murder he was driving his daughter to private school in Tanglewood, then an upscale area of Houston. Washburn had talked with reporters with the condition that his two children not be named or involved in the San Angelo case. The Post also recounted the Coke County attempted extortion case against Washburn, which had been dropped. It was because of that Coke County incident that Papa had said on the day of the murder, "Find out where Harry Washburn has been in the last 24 hours."[66]

Washburn downplayed the 1951 indictment, telling Houston reporters that the incident was exaggerated by Mr. Weaver and that the charges were ridiculous and that is why they were dropped. Washburn went on to tell reporters that, after the charges were dropped, the Weavers made a cash settlement of $30,000. with him to waive any and all rights to a claim against my mother's eventual estate. The last point that the article makes is that Washburn only lost his cool once during the interview when he was told that Weaver had said that he might have seen Washburn in a store during his stay in Houston just before the murder. Washburn is quoted as saying, "I know I didn't see Harry Weaver in Houston because if I see him any time, I'm going to stomp the living daylights out of him!"[67] So much for letting bygones be bygones.

Another article in the Post on Sunday refers to Aubrey Stokes as the "suspect-switching District Attorney" who had cleared Mr. Harry Weaver of all suspicion in the death of Mrs. Weaver. The article states Washburn was at that time in jail in San Angelo and describes him as, "Harry L. Washburn, 38, a one-man building contractor, lately unemployed, who lives at 43 West Broad Oaks Ave."[68]

From the newspaper accounts it certainly appears that the District Attorney had his entire focus on my Papa as the killer in the first several days of the investigation. However, Mr. Stokes did mention a new lead on Tuesday, January 25th. He went to Houston two days later. In those first few days, I wonder if Harry Washburn thought he was going to get away with murder. Despite the reported focus on a suspect in San Angelo, it now appears that the San Angelo authorities had Washburn in their sights from the beginning. Perhaps the focus on my Papa was a ruse - a distraction that even Ranger Rohatsch was a part of when he told Mr. North, the newspaper photographer, that the initial questioning of Washburn had been a "wild goose chase."[69]

Papa was certainly persuaded by the ruse - so much so that he offered the reward 8 days after his wife's death. Those 8 days may have bought the District Attorney time to build a case against Washburn without alerting Washburn to ongoing law enforcement suspicions of only him. The Houston paper states that the arrests came about as a result of the "unrequested cooperation of Houston police in the sensational San Angelo bomb death."[70] A veteran Houston police detective by the name of H.K. Thompson, leading a team of burglary and theft officers, uncovered the information that made possible the warrant for the arrest of Harry Washburn.

D.A. Stokes, Ranger Rohatsch and a Houston Ranger named Oliver drove with Washburn and another suspect to Austin where they were able to use a Department of Public Safety plane to fly to San Angelo. They arrived just after noon on Saturday. Mr. Stokes then made the announcement clearing Mr. Weaver. The San Angelo Standard Times reports that Papa responded to the announcement by saying, "I am sorry for Washburn."[71]

Perhaps others would have thought to express pity for the accused. But I am impressed by Papa's compassion for this man who had already brought such turmoil into his life and the lives of his loved ones. I have no doubt that Papa's expression was sincere. He had introduced my mother to this man, perhaps out of the simple desire to be a good guy toward another man less fortunate than he. Perhaps there were other reasons; they may never be known. It seems that my mother's stepfather was also a victim of Harry Washburn, most likely charmed by the alluring and convincing façade that is so often ingrained in the sociopathic personality. It is hard to imagine what he or my mother and aunt were experiencing during those days of the investigation. The arrest of Harry Washburn must have brought relief – the investigation was over. I wonder what other feelings welled up, threatening to overwhelm, with the knowledge that the killer had been such an intimate part of their own family for a time.

CHAPTER THREE

Evidence

If he has a conscience he will suffer for his mistake.
That will be punishment — as well as the prison.
~Fyodor Dostoyevsky

After the arrest, the intelligence and care that were part of the investigation became even more evident as details of that process emerged in the newspaper. In Houston, Detective Thompson and his associates performed their public safety duties with outstanding results. They interviewed two men, Henry McKinnis and James Ray Fife. Coincidentally, McKinnis at the time was living at 1010 Drew Avenue, apparently just down the street from Papa's Houston rental property. McKinnis and Fife swore that, during the previous spring, Washburn had given them cash and weapons - a shotgun and a pistol - along with a rental car and instructions to go and kill Harry Weaver. Detective Thompson had gotten a tip that McKinnis had been overheard in a bar talking about being hired by Washburn in 1954. Mr. Thompson found McKinnis on Thursday; that led to Fife and then to a man named Carl Henninger.

Police were able to recover the shotgun Henninger had pawned in Houston. McKinnis and Fife had given the shotgun to Henninger when he asked to borrow ten bucks so that his (soon-to-be-estranged) wife could get some decent clothes in order to start working a job that she had been promised. McKinnis and Fife then took Washburn's money, the pistol and the car on a little road trip. In San Antonio, they pawned the pistol in order to continue their drinking spree. They told authorities they had given Washburn the name of a border-town guy who would probably kill Weaver for him for $1,500. After that, they insisted, they had no more to do with Washburn and had absolutely no knowledge of the plan to bomb the car. Henninger had lived with either McKinnis or Fife during the shotgun affair and the road trip but refused to say anything about any of it. The police responded to his lack of cooperation by charging him with murder.

Washburn somehow managed to hire the renowned criminal attorney, Percy Foreman. His first hearing date, the examining trial, was postponed until sometime after February 9th, the earliest date that this famous attorney and the San Angelo District Attorney, Aubrey Stokes, could both be available to attend. Washburn was to be held without bond until then. Percy Foreman discounted all of the mounting evidence as false stories that had been fabricated with the aim of cashing in on some part of the $10,000. reward. The local paper points out that there is no real evidence - only two statements from petty criminals who say that Washburn had previously hired them to commit murder.

At around 5:30 p.m. on Tuesday, with no advance announcement, Henninger got released from jail. A local reporter happened to see Henninger in an airport limousine and spoke with him. The Standard Times reported that Henninger said, "I'm a man with a clear conscience that has nothing to worry about. ... I'm just an innocent man, a victim of circumstances." He then said was anxious to see his "kid" and proceeded to make this cryptic remark about the Houston police: "Those boys are going to see me again. I'll have a good one for you."[72] The paper adds, "He then laughed and declined to amplify the remark."[73] Henninger was due to be subpoenaed as a material witness in the murder case. He and his wife were separated at that time. Who knows what the significance of his allusion to the

Houston police might have been but his disdain for law enforcement rings clear.

McKinnis told officers that four days before Mrs. Weaver's death, he was approached by Washburn with a second request to kill Weaver, this time with a bomb.

In Houston, police were looking at two other men and a 30-year-old woman whom they believed could shed light on the case. On Thursday, February 3rd, the underlying facts of the case and theories about its perpetrators hit the papers. The local headline read, "'Know Who Did It Cops Say In Bombing." A sub-headline at the left says, "Dynamite Expert Talks In Houston."[74] The article quotes Houston Police Chief Jack Heard as saying, "We now know who set the bomb. ... Information from the ex-convict, Andrew H. Nelson, 45, of Houston, touched off a search for wire and dynamite caps in Rosenberg, Tex."[75] Nelson reportedly told police about taking "another man"[76] to the small town of Rosenberg, 30 miles southwest of Houston, to buy dynamite. Then Nelson took him into a wooded area to show him "how to make and connect the bomb. ... Nelson told police his companion went to San Angelo the night before the slaying and hooked up the explosives, intending to kill Mrs. Weaver's husband."[77]

Nelson had been arrested in Houston on Sunday, January 30th. He was charged with the $7,428. burglary of a Houston market. It appears that he was still in custody for that crime when he made his statement to police on Wednesday, February 2nd, two weeks after the bombing.

On Friday the 4th, another strand of the story began to unravel. "Woman Wrestler Reports 'Extortion Plot' In Bombing" was the headline in the local paper and, just to the right, a sub headline read, "$10,000 To Kill Weaver Rejected."[78] This twist in the story concerns a 24 year-old woman wrestler, known as Nature Girl, who turned out to be the estranged wife of Henninger. She told police that Washburn had approached her in Houston sometime in 1954 with a plan for her to kill Mr. Weaver.

Mrs. Henninger reportedly said that Washburn "asked her to go to San Angelo, contact Weaver and get into a discussion with him about a gun collection at the Weaver's Coke County ranch home. ... the plan was for her to get Weaver into the backyard at the ranch house and shoot him during a target practice with his collection of pistols. She said the shooting was to have appeared as an accident."[79] She also told police that Washburn told her that Mrs. Weaver "... is an easy touch. If I can get rid of Weaver, his wife will pay off to keep her family from harm."[80] She said Washburn told her he intended to get a first payment of $30,000. from Mrs. Weaver and eventually would get a total of $100,000. Houston police had been looking for Mrs. Henninger for about a week when she showed up and volunteered this information. She said she had met Washburn in April of 1954 through John McKinnis.

Of course, one might wonder what a person should do if approached with a request to commit murder. Mrs. Henninger said that she had told a friend – a merchant seaman – about the offer and that she'd asked him to warn Mr. Weaver. I wonder how many seamen find their way to San Angelo – landlocked and as far away from any big water as just about any Texas town. It probably would not have made a difference. The Weavers already knew what kind of man Washburn was. Her response to the proposal seems a little weak, given the eventual outcome. But it looks like she moved in rough circles and was probably struggling, in her own way, to get by in a world that didn't give much license to women. She was apparently separated from her husband who had just been released from the San Angelo jail. I guess a woman doesn't take too many chances crossing men who have so little regard for the law. Nature Girl left the state to visit a sister and was not called to testify at the Grand Jury.

Various aspects of the case developed quickly and became public information during the additional testimony for the Grand Jury before Judge Joe L. Mays of the 51st District Court.

Houston area law enforcement officers checked details of Andrew Nelson's story about having shown Washburn how to use dynamite and ignite it from a car engine. Houston Chief of Police, Jack Heard, and Detective H. K. Thompson had received tips prior to Nelson's burglary arrest that the former convict was involved in the Weaver case. They had searched for the practice demolition site in the woods around Rosenberg but hadn't found anything of consequence. When they brought Nelson to that area, he pointed out the site of the test explosion. The local paper reports, "The scarred earth was found near a creek and in the vicinity, officers picked up several links of wire. Nelson has told officers he and his companion fired off one shot of dynamite by hooking it with a wire to a car motor during the demolitions test."[81]

Nelson is reported to have said that his companion rigged 60 feet of wire to some dynamite and hooked it to his car engine. Nelson is quoted as having said, "He started the ignition of his auto and the dynamite blew up. ... by this time I figured he wanted the dynamite for something else than blowing up tree stumps like he told me earlier."[82] Nelson also told officers that his companion in the demolition experiment subsequently told him in Houston, "I killed the wrong person."[83]

The investigators needed verification that Nelson and his companion purchased dynamite. They found the clerk who sold the dynamite and caps to Nelson and another man. A waitress was also able to identify Nelson and, from a photo, another suspect as being in Rosenberg that day.

Despite all of this, at the conclusion of testimony for the Grand Jury, District Attorney Stokes told the press that he doubted any charges would be filed against Nelson.

On Friday morning, February 4th, the local paper reported that "... a man carrying the driver's license and credentials of Harry L. Washburn was arrested and fined at 4 a.m. on the morning of January 19th at Columbus, 72 miles west of Houston on a possible route to San Angelo. ... The man was arrested for running a stoplight after a 70 mile-an-hour chase and, according to records, paid a fine after which he presumably continued east toward Houston."[84] Why this detail had not come to light sooner may have something to do with the fact that Washburn was apparently fined that night on the spot and was then allowed to continue on his way. Of course it is possible that D.A. Stokes was aware of this detail long before the press. Or perhaps it just took that long for the news of the explosion and its connection to Washburn to become evident to the officer who ticketed him that night in Columbus.

Washburn was still maintaining his innocence, insisting that he had been in Houston both the night of January 18th and the next morning at the time the bomb exploded in San Angelo. Both of these facts turned out to be true. He just wasn't there during the in-between hours.

By February 5th, the investigation of the case was all but wrapped up. So the local paper found another angle on the story. On Monday the 6th, a sub-headline above the fold read, "Washburn Offered Comforts In Jail."[85] The inmate had to ask for sheets and a pillowcase. When that became public several local citizens came forward to offer a little hospitality. A man paid $12.18 for the sheets and said "I hate to see any man in a spot and friendless."[86] Seven women also came forward to offer home cooking. One woman sent in "a chicken dinner … complete with dressing, pecan pie and cake."[87] Another woman called the jail and said she would bring a chicken dinner over Thursday and another said she would bring cigarettes.

I asked Joe North if this kind of hospitality was common in the San Angelo jail. He didn't recall anything about this aspect of the story. Maybe Washburn's sociopathic magic was working its ways on the good citizens of San Angelo. Joe North did say that Washburn asked him not to take his picture when they were in the jail area. Mr. North obliged.

When he was first arrested, this reflection of either small town policies or how times have changed was recounted in the San Angelo paper. Washburn was taken out of his cell for about one hour by Detective Lee Braziel for fingerprinting, mugging, and then to a West Beauregard Avenue barber shop for a haircut. The local paper states, "Braziel commented later that apparently no one recognized the prisoner."[88] I'm sure justice was served in some small way in that they took his mug shot before they prettied him up at the barber.

Joe North told me that the San Angelo jail at that time consisted of maybe four or five cells in the basement of City Hall. My uncle, E.A. Blackburn, wrote a book about the county jails of Texas: *Wanted: Historic County Jails of Texas*. He wrote that, after some years with highly inadequate facilities, the updated Tom Green County Jail was built in 1884 with a new addition in 1912. He described it as "... a limestone structure with a central tower and crenellations."[89] That addition doubled the cell space and the facility was not renovated again until 1957, two years after Washburn's stay there. Getting out for a haircut was probably a very welcome reprieve from that 70 year-old basement.

About 35 people testified before the Grand Jury. Washburn's attorney, Percy Foreman, had already made his exit from the case after the preliminary hearing. Two local attorneys represented Washburn at the Grand Jury proceedings. Just before it began, the jailer, L. A. Stevens, said that Washburn was "feeling pretty good"[90] after medical treatment for a stomach disorder. I wonder if churning anxiety unleashing acid on the delicate insides of this man with a cool and calculating outside was taking its toll; or was this just another one of his manipulations?

Papa testified. The paper recounted it this way: "A surprise witness ... looking grim and unwilling to speak to newsmen about the case, entered the grand jury room at about 3:50 a.m. An hour and a half later he came out, passing within three feet of Washburn who was waiting to testify. In contrast, Washburn, 38, Houston contractor and former son-in-law to the Weavers, remained in the grand jury room less than 15 minutes."[91]

Nelson was brought from Houston. They questioned him for about 50 minutes and then returned him to the Tom Green County Jail. The Swishers, a married couple who had cared for Washburn's children the night he was arrested, were in the Grand Jury room for about one half hour. San Angelo's small town paper did a thorough job of informing readers of the tiniest details of the day's events at the courthouse. "Fanciest stepping witness was Dr. H.P. Swisher, Jr. of Houston, who twice walked the length of the hall, using District

Attorney, Aubrey D. Stokes, as interference while successfully dodging photographers. Whatever reluctance his wife might have had vanished when the flashgun of a photographer hiding behind a door failed to work. Mrs. Swisher's resulting smile was caught by another photographer whose flash equipment did function."[92] The photo made the paper. Her smile is wide and relaxed and, of course, she is carrying her gloves. There were other pictures too. Nelson is wearing a Western suit, hands in front of him, and looks like he's in handcuffs. There is something about the man that just looks criminal – the angle of his jaw, the stiffness with which he seems to be carrying himself and something intense about the eyes. Washburn, escorted by a man in uniform, thrusts his chin forward a bit and is looking up slightly. The photo exudes cockiness. All of the pictures of Washburn are blurred on the microfiche. I have been grateful to not have a clear image of that man in my head.

Mr. Titel who worked at Southern Sale and Transportation Company sold the dynamite to Nelson and his companion on January 14th. Mrs. Strain and Mrs. Rogers, two women who worked in the ice cream parlor across the street from Mr. Titel's company, testified that on that same day they had seen Nelson and Washburn in the ice cream parlor. Page twelve of Friday's local paper shows a photo of the two women. A tall one is holding a clutch bag and a newspaper; a much shorter woman looks directly into the camera with a mild expression. Just ordinary folks caught up in the biggest story yet to hit San Angelo.

A man who heard the test blasts is shown in another photo. Black and balding, his name is Charlie Brown. He lived near those woods in Rosenberg and testified that he had heard explosions on the day Nelson was there with Washburn.

E.Y. Ginn, the Chief of Police of Columbus, talked about the night he issued a speeding ticket to "a man carrying Washburn's operator's license."[93] When I spoke with Mr. North, he remembered this as having taken place at Rosenberg, Texas. I didn't correct him and he went on to say that a deputy had cited Washburn and, when

Washburn said he didn't have time to stay around to pay the fine, had accepted payment of the fine, in cash, from Washburn.

More tiny details show up as the local paper reports, "All Isn't Grim At Jury Action."[94] When Mr. Weaver left the courtroom he was asked, "How do things look?" He answered, "It looks a lot better than two weeks ago." When asked, "Did you see Washburn in there, Mr. Weaver?" He replied as he took off his glasses, "Was he there? My sight is pretty bad."[95] The Grand Jury proceedings, I believe, were to be kept confidential. Or perhaps Papa just chose not to share.

Police officers stationed at the head of both sets of stairs on the third floor discouraged many would-be spectators. Only newsmen, officers, witnesses and, of course, office workers on the third floor were permitted by the guards to pass. Witnesses were directed to the waiting room at the east end of the third floor. The final paragraph notes that no effort was made to prevent witnesses from talking to reporters. "As one officer pointed out, nearly every phase of the case has been so widely publicized that witnesses could not tell reporters anything new."[96]

The local paper includes more photos. H.K. Thompson, the Houston detective, resembles Spencer Tracy with his black fedora and thick black glasses. The image of Houston Police Captain Cecil Priest is captured from a low angle, giving him a very powerful appearance.

A variety of other people testified:

Margaret Markle, a Houston probation office employee, was an investigator in the child custody action between Washburn and my mother, "his former wife."[97]

Vincent Brady, a route salesman for a Houston dairy, was asked to share whatever it was that he knew about the case. It may have been in keeping with the times for fresh milk to have been delivered to the door of Washburn's home, perhaps very early on the morning he drove back from San Angelo, his children presumably still sleeping in their beds. The details of Brady's testimony were not provided in the paper.

Pawn shop employees gave testimony regarding the pawning of the shotgun by Henninger and the pistol by McKinnis and Fife in San Antonio.

Carroll J. M. Hawkins was the merchant seaman who, according to police, was an acquaintance of Mrs. Henninger.

A Houston bartender, Salvadore Lucido, overheard McKinnis talking about Washburn.

Andrew Nelson's wife, Katherine, testified that she stayed with Washburn's two children while he was away during the night before the explosion. I would guess this testimony pretty much sealed the case.

The court reporter was Harry Edmond. Apparently a machine was brought in to the courtroom, leading the newspaper to speculate that, "Possibly some or all of the testimony was recorded in this manner."[98] I presume that, prior to the arrival of the machine, standard shorthand would have been the prevailing, low-tech, approach to court reporting.

Washburn was indicted on the charge that he did "voluntarily and with malice aforethought kill Helen Harris Weaver by causing a bomb ... to be attached to the electrical system of an automobile."[99]

The local paper reports that Nelson was cited on three parts in one indictment. In addition to murder, he was charged with aiding Washburn "... in the commission and execution of said offense."[100] The third count states that Nelson, "did aid, abet, conspire with and cause Harry L. Washburn to possess ... a bomb ... for the purpose of causing injury to Harry E. Weaver."[101] The indictments describe the bomb as, "a collection of dynamite and electrical detonating caps."[102] The bomb was, "attached to the electrical system of an automobile in such a manner that an attempt to start the motor of said automobile ... would cause an explosion."[103] The indictment further charged that Nelson, "did willfully advise with, prepare and furnish arms and aid to ... Harry L. Washburn."[104] It alleges that Nelson, "did purchase dynamite and electrical detonation caps and did give Harry L. Washburn direction as to where, how and the manner in which the dynamite and caps should be used."[105] Significant was a statement in the indictment that "Nelson was not present at the commission of said offense by the said Harry L. Washburn."[106]

On Sunday morning, Feb 13, 1955, the long awaited headline appears in the San Angelo Standard Times: "Jury Indicts Nelson, Washburn in Bombing."[107] The paper published pictures of each of the accused, larger than before. Nelson looks considerably older and less dashing than he did in his earlier picture as he approached the courthouse several days before. Washburn is turned partially away from the camera. The caption reads, "... unworried, he says."[108]

Deputy Sheriff B.J. Dooley read the indictment and gave copies to each defendant. He is the one who described Washburn as unworried. He stated that Washburn was very interested in the indictment and pointed out some inconsistencies between his copy and that being read in court. Dooley also stated that Washburn asserted that authorities had indicted the wrong people, "... or words to that effect."[109] Nelson didn't seem bothered by the indictment and never even looked at it. He just said "thank you" and put it in his pocket.[110]

Papa's attorney, Carl Runge was unsurprised by the indictments, saying they were "about what we expected."[111] He reminded reporters that one of Weaver's first comments after the death of his wife was, "Find out where Washburn has been the last 24 hours."[112] The local paper also reported that, after the indictments were read, Papa's lawyer's made some comments regarding the reward money. "Runge also said the fact much of the information given the grand jury had been offered before the $10,000 reward was posted would not keep those responsible from receiving the money in the event of final convictions."[113] This sounds like a little I-told-you-so for the District Attorney. When I asked my father about the final disposition of the reward money, he did not recall the details but thought it was likely distributed among several people.

In addition, the local paper mentions that, "On June 11th, 1951, Washburn was charged on indictments alleging attempted burglary, extortion, assault and with attempt to murder Mr. and Mrs. Weaver. At the time those indictments were returned, Washburn was involved in a divorce and custody action with his wife, Mrs. Weaver's daughter.

All three indictments were dismissed March 3rd, 1952 when Mr. and Mrs. Weaver refused to testify and said they no longer desired to prosecute."[114]

I do not know if Nelson was ever prosecuted for his alleged role in facilitating the murder. The San Angelo Standard Times recounted his history, stating that his most recent employment had been as a trainman in Topeka, Kansas. Both the Houston police and the FBI had information on Nelson: he spent time in the federal prison at Leavenworth for the attempted robbery of a post office. By 1952 he had been arrested for a narcotics violation in Albuquerque. But in 1955, at age 43 or 44, he was out, loose, and admitted he was able to teach Washburn how to detonate explosives from a car starter. I wonder how many people with this many strikes against them ever find a path to the straight and narrow. The vindictive part of me believes that those with this kind of track record don't die of old age in their beds surrounded by loved ones. Yet, the compassionate part of me hopes that they do.

The Wednesday, February 16th, Standard Times ran this sub-headline, "Judge Mays Denies Bond to Washburn."[115] At least there was no getting out of county jail for Washburn.

Arraignment took place on February 18th before Judge Joe L. Mays. The judge said efforts were underway to schedule the trials for April or May. Joe North remembered going to Fort Worth to testify in Washburn's trial. But I remember my father receiving an envelope in the mail in the early 1980s with a newspaper article talking about the Waco, Texas trial of Harry Washburn being the first televised trial in the state of Texas. Although one other trial had been filmed, edited and then broadcast, Washburn's trial was the first *live broadcast* of a trial anywhere in the United States. When Washburn was asked if he had concerns about the live television coverage of his trial, his response was described this way, "... a dispassionate Harry L. Washburn remarked before being found guilty of murder: 'Naw, let it go all over the world.' "[116]

The trial brought to light several other interesting aspects of the case. The D.A. had indicated during Grand Jury proceedings that a gas station attendant and a waitress could place Washburn in San Angelo the night before the explosion. I do not know whether they testified at the trial. It seems that the tiny piece of wire that was discovered at the blast site, dangling from the ignition switch, became crucial to the prosecution of the case. Bits and pieces of the same wire were also found in Harry Washburn's garage and at the test site in Rosenburg. Nelson's wife, Katherine, testified that she babysat the two children on the night of the 18th until the morning of the 19th and that Washburn was away from his home all night. The one-way drive to San Angelo was around 400 miles. At an average speed of 50 mph, it would have taken 8 hours. The fact that Washburn was cited and paid a fine for speeding in Columbus during the time he said he was caring for his children in Houston also seems to have been a nail in his coffin.

The guilty verdict came on December 10th, 1955 – my mother's 27th birthday.

CHAPTER FOUR

Victim

*Maybe you don't know what the nights are like for
people who can't sleep. They all feel guilty. What's
past lies still ahead, and the future is finished.*
~Rainer Maria Rilke

Already in her young life, my mother had experienced periods
of what my father described as being "flakey." By that I think
he meant that my mother had times when she perceived reality a
little differently from most people. Her teen years had apparently
involved some excessive moodiness and rebellion. Much later in her
life she was diagnosed with bipolar disorder. If that illness had been
evident earlier in her life, she could have been prone to periods of
depression interspersed with times of excessive energy and agitation
that sometimes show up as a heightened sense of self-importance
and capabilities (grandiosity) or, on the other hand, an agitated,
frightened state of active paranoia.

Knowing that bipolar illness is aggravated by stress, I wonder
how she coped with the news of her former husband's arrest for the
gruesome murder of her mother. My father had travelled to San
Angelo with her as soon as they learned of Helen Harris Weaver's

death. I am sure he had to return to work in Billings soon after; he may even have gone without her several days after the funeral. Also, someone must have been caring for my brother in Billings. A toddler, he certainly needed a parent back with him. I presume my parents had already been planning to have another child. My father told me that I was conceived on their trip to the funeral in San Angelo during those cold January days of 1955.

It is so curious to ponder the facts of one's own conception. I've come to know my father as a man who cared deeply about others. I have no trouble seeing him motivated to add some joy to his own life with another child. Yet I imagine he hoped even more that another child would bring joy to his beloved wife, especially in those days of darkness and grief. Joy, of course, in the form of a new baby. But how much is a fetus impacted by the emotional state of its mother? She was grieving throughout my gestation. I have come to wonder to what extent a fetus senses the feelings of its mother. I've always wondered why I have often felt guilty for things indefinable ever since before I could remember or even name the feeling.

My mother's divorce from Harry Washburn was as messy as they come, with slanderous newspaper accounts - fed to the press by Washburn - of accusations of misdeeds. Washburn's renowned divorce attorney, Percy Foreman, was paid, I am certain, with my mother's family's money. I have no doubt that Washburn clung to custody as a way to maintain his connection to that family wealth. The Houston courts granted primary custody of the two children to Washburn. My mother exercised her visitation rights from her home in San Angelo, before she met my father.

Friends introduced my parents, as they both liked to play bridge. They courted and were planning to marry when my father was transferred to North Dakota. Mother moved in with some friends in Williston, North Dakota while they continued their courting. Williston was in the middle of an oil boom and rental property was hard to find. However, after they got married in Bismarck, they sort of inherited a rental - a farm house owned by a Mr. Strand - from a co-worker who was leaving the area. Nana sent my mother's furnishings; Helen and Roy set up house.

Mother continued to exercise visitation rights, picking up the children without alerting Washburn to her whereabouts. The visitation schedule was probably something like a week or two every 3 months. She simply took the children back to San Angelo for their father to drive from Houston and pick them up, as usual. I remember mother saying that the children would arrive from Houston all out of sorts, having had no routine, no regular meals or bedtimes and that sort of thing. She said their father would tell them horrible things like their new stepfather (my father) was going to kill them. I have a very vague memory of my mother talking of a time when Washburn tied my sister to her bed with the bologna sandwich she had declined at lunch, having been told she would be staying there until she ate the food that was offered. Maybe parenting should require a license.

Washburn eventually figured out they were living out of state. At some point he went to Montana to pick up the two children for a visit and never returned them. Mother got legal advice that produced very little in the way of legal recourse. My parents and everyone else in the family agreed that this was just one of Washburn's manipulations aimed at getting money from the family. My father told me that my mother consulted with her mother and her mother's attorney in San Angelo. They all agreed that giving Washburn full responsibility for the children would be a way to call his bluff - as long as no one gave him any money. At this point, Washburn had most likely already confronted Papa and Nana at the ranch house and then allegedly had been paid $30,000. for an agreement to not pursue any further claim to my mother's future inheritance. The thinking was that, if no one gave him any more money, Washburn would eventually tire of the struggles of parenting and return custody to my mother. But it seems that Washburn just farmed the children out to his sister, his neighbors and whomever else he could find to watch them. When he was arrested, Washburn claimed that Nana had sent $500. in cash for the children. Who knows if she really did, but that certainly would have undermined the original intention of my mother's decision to relinquish custody. I do not know if evidence of other payments to Washburn surfaced as part of his murder trial. My father emphasized the reluctance with which my mother agreed to this plan to call his bluff. It was probably the details of the legality of this custody arrangement that caused the two children to be placed in foster care and then with my aunt for a time, instead of being promptly returned to my mother when Washburn was arrested.

I am certain that Washburn made life hell for my mother any way that he could. I believe that Washburn considered these children his very lifeline, his only remaining connection to an income stream that would support his lifestyle without requiring the nuisance of a job.

In those early days of her grief, I wonder how my mother saw the situation. Despite her independent character, I think she was reliant on my father in general and probably felt very alone, even in the company of her family members, all of whom were grieving themselves. According to my father, she was already pregnant, but likely not aware of it. I imagine she had a few drinks during those long evenings of shock and uncertainty. Papa had always known, and I imagine she did too, that Washburn was somehow responsible. I wonder if they spoke of it. Or was it their elephant in the living room - a subject made too painful for words by their connection to the perpetrator of the heinous crime? My mother, the ex-wife, one bridge between this criminal and the innocent life he took, and Papa, the good-intentioned, who introduced them.

Washburn had told Houston Post reporters about the settlement with the Weavers whereby he was paid $30,000. to release any claim to my mother's eventual inheritance. The payment was made to Washburn sometime after the confrontation at the Coke County ranch house in 1951. It came after the charges of attempted extortion were dropped by the Weavers. In January of 1955, it would seem that Washburn was not hurting for money, at least not yet. He had given money to McKinnis and Fife - perhaps as much as $7,500. - a very substantial sum. He lived in a wealthy section of Houston, albeit in an "odd-looking"[117] house. His children attended private schools. Yet Washburn was described by the papers as, "a contractor, lately unemployed."[118] Somewhere in all of these accounts, I read that he had run for County Commissioner at one time but didn't get elected. If he had gotten himself a public position, he probably could have managed to create an illegal income stream with as much potential – or a whole lot more – than my grandmother's deep pockets and tender heart. (I think it is more likely that someone along the way confused this Washburn with the well-regarded Harry Washburn who was a civic leader in Houston.)

It seems evident to me that Washburn was accustomed to his lifestyle and had no way of supporting it. He was likely running out of money and may have felt he was out of time to guarantee access to money from my grandmother after his $30,000. settlement ran out. The cunning and charisma that comes with the sociopathic personality must have been in high gear. Fortunately those traits were not combined with high intelligence. I am sure he was confident that he could manipulate my grandmother as long as her husband was not in the picture. He just wasn't smart enough to commit a murder and get away with it.

Instead, Harry Washburn was in a small cell in the basement of the Tom Green County Courthouse with the sobering knowledge that he had killed the wrong person. His famous lawyer, Mr. Percy Foreman, had abandoned him for lack of funds.

The paper says that Foreman had been representing Washburn "because he feels sorry for him and because two years ago, when he represented Washburn at a child custody hearing, he came to admire Washburn's devotion to his children."[119] Foreman is quoted as saying, "I never did think he was guilty. ... You'll find all kinds of sharks snapping at bait if it's thrown into the ocean."[120] A reference, I presume, to the $10,000. reward.

I struggle against my own feelings of contempt in response to Mr. Foreman's comment on Washburn's dedication to his children. I have no doubt that Washburn's dedication to those children was nothing more than his desperation to cling to the promise of family wealth he thought was guaranteed when he married my mother. Much later, during the trial or one of the many appeals, Washburn's attorney is pictured in the paper with those same two children on his lap in what seems to me to be a disgusting attempt to garner sympathy for a murderer.

Washburn won an appeal due to technicalities regarding the testimony given by Nelson, the detonation accomplice, and the search of Washburn's garage, where law-enforcement officers discovered some of the detonation wire. The search was never thrown out. Finally, in 1957, the original guilty verdict was upheld and Washburn went to prison for life.

I looked into the trial, in a very cursory way, long after my original review of microfiche newspaper articles about the crime. The internet offered several summaries. Much of it was information I either knew or had gleaned through the years. I was startled though – jolted even – to learn that the guilty verdict was reported on my mother's birthday. I do not know if she attended the trial; I think probably not. Her family members likely kept her informed. She also probably could have found news about the trial in the local paper in Billings, if she chose to look. Perhaps she had access to the television coverage of the trial but I do not know how widely that was broadcasted. I am sure she knew of the verdict – most likely the day it was delivered – one day *before* it was reported in the papers. It makes sense now. Hers was the only family birthday that was not celebrated much. I always thought that was just because it fell so close to Christmas.

My mother's decision to marry the monster that was Harry Washburn colored her life thereafter. I believe that, over time and with the added burden of alcoholism, she passively allowed those tints and hues to destroy her. Yet all she was doing was that which was expected of her – to marry and raise a family. Her story unfolded in a time with such limited opportunities for most women. But it is a tragic reminder of our basic responsibility to know ourselves, to remain true to ourselves and to do what we can to make our decisions from choice rather than from obligation. This is easier said than done; it is also much easier in my lifetime than it was in hers. Her story underscores the truth that if we choose to marry, the decision of whom to marry is among the most important ones we will make. That was as true in the 1950s as it is today.

CHAPTER FIVE

Roots

*Although we are driven by forces that are beyond our control
and awareness, we are also the active authors of our fate.*
~Judith Viorst

In the aftermath of her mother's murder, my mother Helen was having a very difficult time emotionally. My father, Roy, tells me that he remained in San Angelo with her and her family for some time after Nana's death. I do not know whether he had returned to his job in Billings when Washburn was arrested. In my mind, I picture Helen alone in Texas, albeit with her stepfather and sister, when the arrest took place in Houston. How terrifying it must be to know that someone with whom you have shared so intimately has the ability to kill another human being. How vulnerable she must have felt. I wonder if she knew, in the way that mothers know, that she had recently become pregnant with me. Just over nine months later was my birthday, after her short labor in twilight sleep, in Billings.

My mother was not coping well with the overwhelming stress by the time she left San Angelo. My father tells me she was very frightened during her airplane trip back to Billings. She became convinced that her coffee had been drugged in an attempt to kill her. She even saved some of the coffee on a napkin and planned to ask my uncle, a physician, to have it evaluated.

In Billings, she entered a psychiatric hospital for a stay. I don't know whether she had ever been admitted before but it was one of several stays of varying duration over the years. Though the terminology to describe psychiatric concerns has changed since those days, it appears that she was so severely depressed that she lost touch with reality. Psychotic Depression. I don't know if she was having visual hallucinations; I don't know if she was feeling desperate or suicidal at that time. She may have been admitted against her will, likely on the order of a doctor in Billings. The criteria for involuntary psychiatric hospitalization were very different in the mid-1950s. For a long time in many states, all that was required was the signature of a spouse and a doctor's order for hospital admission that deprived the individual of their civil rights, sometimes for extended periods of time. Those laws have changed; now an initial evaluation by a specially trained mental health professional is generally required for an initial involuntary stay of short duration - usually a maximum of 72 hours - at a psychiatric facility for observation. Extension of an involuntary stay beyond three days usually involves a court order.

I have no idea how long she was in the hospital that time. Nor do I know whether she was yet aware that she was pregnant with me during the stay. I think that must have been discovered through lab testing that would have been required of all new patients. In the interesting way of memory versus confabulation, I have arrived at my belief that she was taking Valium, either before, during or even after her hospital stay. My father may have told me this. Or I may have gleaned it from her diagnosis. Valium was the miracle drug of that decade, designed to ease the mind and help a person conveniently disregard all things troubling. It was fairly new on the market and may have been the vanguard of an array of miracle medicines to treat psychiatric problems that would be coming to the market over the next several decades. What may not have been known then is that it can have an unwanted effect on the developing fetus in the patient. Nearly forty years later, as I was sitting in a graduate seminar on human development, I learned that Valium is considered a teratogen – a substance likely to cause birth defects – especially in the first trimester of a developing fetus.[121] Cleft palate is one birth defect that is commonly associated with Valium.

So, in November of 1955, I slipped into this world and took my first breath of air with no roof to my mouth. The palate, or roof of my mouth, had failed to form and was split or "cleft". Usually in such circumstances, the lip also fails to form completely. I'm sure my parents were as grateful as I am that my face and lips were complete. The doctors in Billings said to wait until I was three to have the plastic surgery to repair the defect. My father says it was a little difficult to feed me since formula kept coming out of my nose. Other than that, no problems were apparent until I started to talk, probably around age one. Another medical consultant recommended surgery right away, before I was two.

When I learned, at nearly age forty, of the likely role of Valium in my fetal development, I felt extremely angry and was quick to direct that anger at my mother. My outraged thought was, "How could she take a drug that hurt me this way?" It didn't take too long for me to let that anger go. I already knew how deeply she had been suffering in those times. I have come to assume that either medical science was not yet aware of the ill effects of Valium on the developing fetus or else the risk was deemed acceptable given the reward of calming my mother's troubled soul, perhaps even saving her life.

Mother used to tell the story of my homecoming from the hospital as an infant. She said she laid me out on the floor on a blanket for "all the family to see." That memory comes to me even now as a visual picture though I know I have made it up. I see a baby on the blanket with my two brothers, my sister and my father standing around smiling. Even the little dog, Kinker, is excited and bouncing around. I don't actually recall whether Mother ever said they were all there. However, as I have come to understand more about Mother's first two children, they could not have been present that day. Her first two children were in foster care, dictated by the courts. They may have been with their paternal aunt, Mrs. Douty.

I know they spent some time with our maternal aunt as well. But I believe they also received care from strangers and the two of them may even have gone to different homes. It took some time and legal maneuvering to get them returned to my mother.

I know that we were a family of six before I turned three. I remember my mother's passport, with all four children in the picture with her. That was a standard way to issue passports for children in those days. We needed the passport for all of us when my father's work took our family to Tehran, Iran. He'd been promoted to an upper management or perhaps an executive role in oil exploration in the Persian Gulf region. I am sure he was thrilled to be stationed abroad; his wanderlust was always apparent, though subtle. I wonder if he also simply wanted to move us as far away from the tragedy as possible.

I have a copy of the grainy 16mm home movie of a birthday party in the backyard of the house we occupied in Tehran. Modern design with clean lines, the back of the house had a balcony which looked out over the wide lawn with a rectangular pool that no one could swim in because the birds had made it their home. A local woman was hired to cook for us; a man was hired as driver. Whether he was a driver or more of a chauffeur, I don't know. Perhaps these household helpers were extravagances known only to the wealthy in Iran. Or maybe their involvement in our lives was more of a practical necessity of working and living with children in a foreign land. I imagine it was very helpful to be able to rely on a driver who knew the roads and understood the local culture; and a cook who knew the markets and the fair value of household goods. My mother, though, never liked to cook and always had household helpers. That was the way she grew up, so it must have seemed very normal to her to have assistants.

One evening, my parents were returning home from a weekend trip when the driver fell asleep at the wheel. The crash broke my mother's arm. She had been in one car wreck before, when she was a teen in Houston. That left her with a large scar under her right cheekbone. She had cut her face when her head started to go through the windshield or maybe the side "wing" window. A few years ago, my Aunt Sadie Gwin sent me a photo of Mother as a girl, maybe age 15 or 16. It was the first time I had ever seen her without that scar on her cheek. She was so young, beaming and beautiful. The bright spark in her eyes was actually a little bit startling, compared to the other images of her as an older teen, when the darkness had already begun to intrude and diminish the brilliance in her.

Mother's broken arm healed and a new driver was hired. He continued in my parents' employment until we left Iran. Then he maintained contact with our family for several years after. I remember seeing a Christmas card when I was 9 or 10 and back in Texas. He wrote in English and had signed his name in small tight cursive letters of blue ink. The clarity and the very blue-ness of the ink are as vibrant in my memory now as they were in my perception way back then.

At some point during our time in Iran, probably in about 1958, Mother had to travel to the U.S. to tend to some details of Nana's estate. In order to travel without her children, Mother's passport had to be updated to an individual document that did not include her children. This meant that each of the four children had to get an individual passport as well. I still have one of the tiny passport pictures of me as a frail-looking white-haired girl, brow knitted, confused - suspicious perhaps - with eyes focused right into the camera lens. I wonder what I understood at around age three about the goings on in my world. I wonder if I knew my mother was leaving. I wonder if I thought it was my fault, as children tend to do. I wonder if, by then, the hired driver was already trying to take advantage of my innocence and I didn't know how to tell anyone.

One day, as my siblings and I were in the car going from one place to another, the hired driver went around a corner slowly. One of the doors opened and I went tumbling out. That story, told occasionally around the dinner table in later years, usually brought a chuckle from everyone. It always caused me to wonder how that happened. As an adult, when I asked, my father told me that he and Mom had looked me over very carefully. I did not appear to be hurt and the driver continued to be entrusted with taking us all where we needed to go. I had no recollection of any mistreatment by him until my thirties when I came to wonder if my exit from the car that day was perhaps the only way I could express what I could not yet say in words: "I need to get away from this bad man."

I am sure that at the time, my parents had no idea that sexual abuse even happened to children. The mandatory reporting of child abuse became U.S. law in most states in the mid-1980s. Since then, vast amounts of information as well as prevention and treatment strategies have become available to the public. Before then, however, sexual abuse was totally shame-laden and was simply not discussed openly. I think it was considered very rare and thought to be committed by perverts and creeps, not everyday people who might enter into one's own life as employees or even friends of the family.

Too often victims of child rape and molestation were - and often still are - simply not believed even when they muster the courage to come forward and speak up. Re-victimization comes in the form of accusations of attention seeking or lying. That this continues to happen is an unmeasured tragedy in our society. The impact of this harm to children reverberates throughout society in the emotional troubles of those who go without treatment, the health problems that manifest when emotional troubles go unaddressed and the spiritual wounding of souls seeking expansion.

Not long after my mother arrived alone back in the United States, she began to struggle once again with emotional concerns. It is a natural response, when grieving, to feel somehow responsible for the death of our loved one. We wonder what we could have done to change the unwanted outcome. We bargain with God, asking what *could* we have done better to have avoided the awful loss. We ask ourselves, what *should* we have done differently that could have allowed us to avert the now irreversible absence of that one so dear to us. This activity of bargaining represents movement toward the eventual, soothing awareness that what is done is in the past; that whatever we could or should have done is now moot because the time of opportunity for different action has passed. Feeling all the feelings associated with that in order to arrive at a peaceful place of acceptance is the journey of grief. It is as different for each person as the rhythms of our breathing and the textures of our souls.[122]

In Houston, working with my Aunt Sadie Gwin, my mother had to look squarely at the facts involved in settling their mother's estate. The extent to which Mother would benefit financially from the brutality of her first husband's crime must have unleashed a torrent of despair. I am sure her sense of responsibility for her mother's death went way beyond ordinary bargaining. She had complied with her parents' wishes for her to marry Washburn. I believe she picked up and carried a burden of guilt for his actions. So I came to understand that, for her, the activity of bargaining never helped her arrive at that peaceful place of realizing and accepting that there had been nothing she could have done to prevent or change the outcome. I believe the bargaining process brought her, instead, always back to the overwhelming guilt of her misplaced sense of personal responsibility for her mother's death.

My aunt assures me that no one in the family blamed my mother for Nana's death. I believe that to be true, mostly. My mother certainly seemed to blame herself and, I believe, that added fuel to the depression that was already idling within her, erupting at times and then submerging again for varying amounts of time. As the details of the division of assets from Nana's estate began to emerge, it became evident that my mother's inheritance would include lucrative mineral rights and a great deal of land with reservoirs of oil beneath it.

So the tragedy for which my mother felt responsible would also give rise to her inheritance of valuable assets with life-long income-producing potential, if managed carefully. How can one weigh the wealth against the guilt? How does that scale ever settle into balance?

This was my mother's bittersweet inheritance. Any burden of guilt, trivial or huge, brings with it the responsibility to heal it. I hold that this kind of healing is the true spiritual basis of the calling or vocation we each choose. Healing such a deeply wounded soul would, indeed, be a standout accomplishment for anyone. I know my mother tried. She may have partially succeeded for several years, living a sort of happy life as her children were growing up. But I think it was the weight of that guilt that eventually buried any lasting enjoyment of the carefree lifestyle that the assets offered her.

Out of balance emotionally, my mother's disintegration while she was in Houston is no surprise. She began to lose touch with reality again while she was staying with my aunt. The extreme stress of even comprehending her bittersweet inheritance most likely aggravated an already present mental illness - the probable bipolar disorder that seems to have predated her mother's death. She was in need of psychiatric care in Houston. But instead of getting that care, she got on a plane to get back to her husband. The trip to Iran was long and grueling. She was probably already exhausted and stressed. After taking off, probably from New York, she was acting so strangely on the plane that airline officials prevented her from continuing her journey. During a scheduled stop in Amsterdam, Mother was checked in to a hotel where she stayed while airline personnel contacted my father to tell him she needed medical attention and would not be able to fly alone.

I can't imagine how she must have been viewed by the flight personnel. The general public knew so little about depression, especially manic depression, which can cause enormous disruption in a person's perception of reality. Deep fearfulness emerges and drives erratic behavior. Reason goes offline. The stigma associated with mental illness during the 1950s was probably only slightly less than it had been a hundred years earlier when "the insane" were simply locked away, sometimes in chains. It is likely that mother was, once again, having paranoid delusions or thoughts that someone was trying to harm her. Perhaps she was even suspicious of the flight personnel - the very people charged with assisting her while on the plane. She was probably drinking alcohol as well, which could have calmed her agitated mind temporarily, but may also have further disrupted her judgment.

My father, who had been holding down his job and caring for four children in a foreign country, albeit with the help of various household staff, must have left on very short notice. Roy went to Amsterdam to see about Helen. She was in a hotel and had been seen by a doctor. She was considered in need of ongoing psychiatric care. There they were, my parents, as far from home as they were from Iran. My father, alone, confronted the conundrum that life placed before them, as Mother was not lucid. Roy was a talented scientist with a prime geophysics assignment overseas. Mother's health situation demanded a resolution in the very short term. Dutch doctors assured him that, in Tehran, my mother would get the most current psychiatric treatments available. So they returned to Iran. Mother was seen there by a psychiatrist. Years later I found a typed sheet of paper with those awful words, "Psychotic Depression."

I remember reading those words just as I was beginning my graduate training as a mental health counselor. The words barely registered, even though I knew what they meant. The fact that she had suffered from depression throughout her life was certainly no secret. But the word "psychotic" shocked me. I had never seen my mother acting as though she were hallucinating, or responding to voices in her head that only she could hear, or mumbling nonsense while apparently unaware of my presence. Yet that was what psychotic meant to me at the time. Later I would learn about and then help treat depression that is so severe that it leaves people misperceiving reality. I arrived at a better understanding of the nuances of psychosis and mania.

Mother was treated with insulin shock therapy, the precursor to electro-convulsive therapy or ECT. Injections of insulin were given to create a brain seizure that left a patient feeling some relief from depression - for reasons unknown. The procedure itself would have been frightening enough. She was probably strapped on a gurney, perhaps with a mouthpiece to prevent chomping down on the tongue or lips. I envision my mother surrounded by people who were foreign to her, gowned medical personnel perhaps behind white masks, all speaking a foreign language. It seems absolutely terrifying. My mother, of course, never spoke to me of those times. My father hesitantly shared much of this information as I was dealing with my own struggles with depression as an adult many years later.

After about six months in Tehran, the psychiatrist determined that my mother would be better off in a place that was familiar to her. Based on that, my parents made the decision to return to the small city where they had met – my mother's hometown of San Angelo, Texas. When I first learned of that development, I wondered whether the psychiatrist really understood that his advice was sending my mother back to the town where her mother had been murdered. But as my understanding of PTSD (Post Traumatic Stress Disorder) grew, I realized how this move was conceived to be helpful. Facing the huge stressor of going past the site of her mother's murder, the "death scene," should have been good medicine for overcoming the residual trauma. Face the fear and move through it. That would have been the plan. At least my mother was well known in San Angelo and genuinely loved by many people there. The immediate task before her was to forgive herself, to absolve herself of responsibility for that thing that she did not do. The only way out is through.

CHAPTER SIX

Fissure

Growing up means gaining the wisdom and skills to get what we want within the limitations imposed by reality – a reality which consists of diminished powers, restricted freedoms and, with the people we love, imperfect connections.
~Judith Viorst

So my father "retired" from the oil business to return to San Angelo. His company probably would have moved him to New York City, but my parents had no desire for that lifestyle. At around age thirty, my father let go of the career he had trained for. Family belongings were packed into a huge wooden crate that was shipped on a slow boat from the other side of the world to our humble abode in West Texas. That crate became a playhouse for us in the carport of the Village Apartments where we lived. My father became an investor, bought real estate and traded in the stock market. Our lives settled into a routine and, it would seem, many of the troubles went underground - at least for a time.

I had a bedroom of my own with the head of my bed up against a window. The West Texas Winter blew in from the north bringing the chill of the Rocky Mountains with it. It would seep and creep in through the very panes of glass and find its way around the custom-made curves of the headboard that came from Gran's house. That house - the one where my Nana died - was eventually sold and a bank was built in its place. I don't know when. I don't know for how long after they returned to San Angelo my mother had to drive by the "death scene" or else go out of her way to avoid it. But my cousin remembers living there and playing with my sister for some time after Nana's death.

I was blissfully unaware of any other reminders of the tragedy there may have been. I was busy being a child. Shortly after we got settled in San Angelo, I remember a time when I was very frightened by the roar of thunder. In the late summers, usually in the late afternoon, thunderheads would build up in the west. The storms could be terrible there on the western edge of Tornado Alley. I remember towering black clouds filling the sky while the wind whipped strands of hair across my face and then the eerie stillness that came before the storm burst forth.

One day, when I was about four or five, my mother scooped me up and we stood, with my father at her side, on our little front porch looking up into the massive dark clouds. They seemed to take up the entire West. Way up at the top of the clouds, streamers of sunlight shined out from behind and gave the sky a crown to wear. My mother was warm and calm and seemed mesmerized or somehow awestruck by the scene. "How beautiful it is!" she said. In that moment, I came to agree with her. I have loved storms ever since. This memory stands out as my first one. This is also one of the few times I recall a cozy feeling of safety. I know there were others; I just don't remember them.

That closeness, in imagery and feeling, becomes more pronounced each time I remember it. Over the years my memory of that moment has come to fill me with the warm glow of truly knowing that I was loved. Tucked into my mother's arms and resting securely on her hip, looking up at that magnificent sky, light emanating from the darkness - it was something of a mystical experience for me. I didn't have words to describe it then, but I think I knew that I was in the presence of raw creative force. Grace is a word that at least partly describes the peace and security of that moment. In so many ways, as my life was to unfold, that presence has been with me. Even when I was making foolish choices for myself, grace surrounded me, protecting me and perhaps even preparing me for something.

I was probably six when I first went with my mother to the library. Using phonics, she had taught me to read even before the first grade. I vaguely remember getting my library card. When the librarian asked my father's occupation I said he was "unemployed." My mother was quick to provide the correct answer – self-employed. That became one of those family stories that got repeated now and then, much to everyone else's amusement.

By the time I turned eight, we had moved into our home on Montecito Drive. It bordered a city park with a creek running through it. Up in the trees that lined one side of the creek, my brother and I found a crook in the tree with two limbs forming a large V. Thick vines stretched from one branch to the next with lots of supporting vines crisscrossing the area, forming a kind of bed suspended in the air. I still feel the sun on my face when I think of how many hours we spent there – reading or chatting – with the sound of the trickling creek in our ears and the occasional sight of a car passing slowly by the park. No one drove fast then, or so it seemed.

The elementary school was a few blocks away. We generally walked to and from school with never a concern for our safety. In the fall of 1963, my brother, Jamie, was home from school, sick with something minor and watching TV in the children's playroom above the garage. When the news that JFK had died came on the TV, Jamie went into the next room, Dad's home office, to tell him. Jamie got scolded for making things up.

I was at school that day, in second grade. I heard that the news had made the other second grade teacher cry right in front of her class. To me, this was a sign that something was certainly terribly wrong. I can practically see myself sitting at my little desk trying to imagine what it was like to be in that other room where the teacher was crying. Teachers never cried. It was very unsettling. Something heavy and opaque was settling over all of us. It was my first inkling of human death.

I remember the funeral being held on a Saturday but it actually took place on a Monday. So I guess schools were closed that day. I was home and I spent the whole morning watching the procession and the service. I was like most second-graders, completely ignorant of politics. Yet the depth of meaning in the funeral was not wasted on me, even at my young age - the solemn cortege with the riderless horse, Jackie's heavy black veil and little John John's lonely salute. My sense of that day is deeply melancholy still. I visited JFK's gravesite twenty-five years later, at a time in my life when my interest in spiritual realities beyond our physical world was new. I could actually feel the grief in the air around the site as I sat staring into the eternal flame. A nation of mourners had stood on that ground, weeping. I was moved to my knees with tears flowing down as I toppled into that collective chasm of sorrow. It seemed to me then, in the late 1980s, that our country had been bereft of vision for too long. I was frankly surprised by my response to the gravesite. Even the subsequent press about JFK - his sexual exploits, his interesting use of prescription medications and the whole deception of the people with his "family man" aura - hasn't really dampened my respect for the man who inspired us so in his inaugural address.

"Let the word go forth from this time and place, to friend and foe alike, that the torch has been passed to a new generation of Americans. ... unwilling to witness or permit the slow undoing of those human rights to which this Nation has always been committed ... . If a free society cannot help the many who are poor, it cannot save the few who are rich. ... The energy, the faith, the devotion which we bring to this endeavor will light our country and all who serve it - and the glow from that fire can truly light the world."[123]

I don't recall any particular conversations about the assassination in our family. Dallas was not very far away, though. If a leader can be gunned down, what else could happen without warning? I don't recall a conscious decision on my part, but I suspect I simply shifted my focus to things within my control. School was generally easy for me. Good grades got me some acknowledgement so I was happy to comply. I didn't miss a single day of school that year and I still have the report cards that show it. I don't recall anyone telling me about my grandmother and her perfect attendance. I do remember being acknowledged for it at school but not so much at home. It was just expected.

I was aware, even then, of the privileged status I held within our community. It came not just with the assets, but also with our family name and heritage. I think mother made an effort to keep us humble. She told a story of a young girl from another family who had been on a train and was unhappy with the accommodations. When telling her father about it later, the girl said, "Daddy, I almost had to tell them who I was!" The father must have smiled a little when he replied, "And who was ya, honey?" That story always made my mother laugh out loud.

We were taught to value our ancestry and, like our ancestors, value the land itself. But wealth often brings changes in attitudes and changes in values. Mother told me the story of the pearl necklace she occasionally wore. It was a pendant with one nickel-sized, freshwater pearl wrapped in a gold frame, reportedly designed by Tiffany & Co. of New York, or so the story went. When Ralph Harris gave it to his wife, Sadie, she supposedly threw it back at him and said something like, "I'm not going to wear those old pearls out of the Concho River!" The pearl is a thing of rare beauty and is still in the family. It is not marked in any way to reflect it having been set by Tiffany though. DNA testing suggests it came from the San Saba River, not the Concho in San Angelo.

During fourth grade, I developed a strange medical condition that caused intense headaches that magically disappeared at 3 p.m. On those days, I would often ride with Mother to the ranch. It was a forty-five minute drive one way. I loved to draw as a girl and remember being in the car, adding foliage to a tree by laying the pencil on its side and rubbing lots of lead onto the page. Mother must have been distracted by my motions or the sound it made. She glanced over and was a little harsh when she said that I was using up my lead and there wasn't a sharpener. Many years later as I remembered that day, I realized that I had taken her comment as criticism of my art work. My enthusiasm for drawing waned after that. Now it is simple to see that she was doing that motherly thing of anticipating problems and trying to prevent them - trying to control life for her daughter and for herself.

I am so grateful I have had the guidance and the will to uncover and release these misconceptions from childhood. Our conditioning from childhood comes about in these small ways and so often becomes the source of our adult life troubles. Finding the connection is the tricky part; healing it is each person's responsibility. Blaming our parents may be a phase we go through but it is certainly not the end of the journey. More the beginning, really.

By fifth grade I had developed a deep friendship with a boy named David. I remember sitting next to him in class and eventually we traded disks. That was our little fad gold- or silver-colored disks with our names engraved on them; we wore them on long chains. David lived near us, on Paseo de Vaca, in the old established neighborhood not far from downtown. (That wide street once was the "paseo" where cattle were driven to market down the middle of the street.) He invited me to go with him to the park one day – the park by my house. We came upon a strange looking creature staring at us through the trees across the creek. It was about 20 feet away. Small, like a stuffed bear, it had large eyes with highly contrasting marks around them which made the eyes seem even bigger. Its ears lay flat, kind of molded to the side of its head. It was gray and brown, mostly, and blended in with the underbrush. I remember sitting and being utterly fascinated by this, not fearful at all. We could not identify the creature and I wonder if it wasn't some kind of prank. If he and perhaps a friend were trying to scare me, they didn't realize how secure I felt when I was with David.

My parents had become ranchers. They were also some of the very few Republicans in West Texas and, to hear them tell it, in the entire state of Texas at that time. When George Bush, Sr. was running for Congress, my parents held a fundraiser on the large terrace of our home. I remember tasting beer that came from the tap that was set up out there. Mr. Bush was due to fly out that night to San Antonio but he was delayed when, on the way to the airport, he came across a car accident and stopped to help. Mr. Bush missed the last plane out that night and returned to our house to spend the night in my oldest brother's room at the end of the upstairs hall. My father, an experienced private pilot with a plane, would fly him to San Antonio the following morning in time for Mr. Bush's next campaign stop. As the story goes, my father was walking down the hall the next morning to wake him when he saw Mr. Bush heading across the hall to the bathroom, stark naked! I think it must be true. My father was not one to make up stories. I wonder if Mr. Bush even had a suitcase with him for his quick trip to San Angelo. I also wonder how many politicians of today would have stopped to help.

Our weekends were devoted to ranching. My siblings and I all had jobs and recreation we enjoyed at the ranch. We experienced amazing things there. I saw a calf being born that was encased in a sack - typical for cows I guess, but very bizarre to me. My father and brothers learned how to weld in order to build holding pens for cattle. We rode on roundup though I was too young and lacking in riding skills to be much help. I was still afraid of the horse, but only when I was on top of it. I loved brushing them and being with them. Riding one day on my mare with her new foal at her side, I was taken on a wild ride through thick trees when the foal took off and her mother didn't think twice about following her. I held on low, so that the horse's own forehead broke the branches. Finally I jumped off. I was roughed up and shaken. Nobody made me get back on the horse that day and I wish they had.

We seemed to be a happy family. I think my mother hit her stride in those years. When she stepped into *her* mother's ranching shoes, her connection with that land and with her ancestors came alive. That may have healed her as much as anything. She brought science to the livelihood of cattle ranching by tagging the cows' ears and fertility-testing them. She brought art as well, singing to the cows to calm them as we drove through the herds in wintertime with food on the tailgate of the huge old pickup that we called the Green Monster. In many ways my mother seemed a part of that land. And when I think of her happy times, they usually are memories of those ranch years. I think my mother's heart was broken when the rumors began to circulate that the family ranchland would be condemned to make way for a lake. Although the lake would bring water to the surrounding communities, the loss of that land took with it some part of her that never resurfaced.

On town days she played bridge. At that time I had no idea how instrumental her Gran, Sadie, had been in bringing the game of bridge to San Angelo. I suspect my mother knew that she was carrying on the tradition of gaming and socializing that had been so integral to Sadie Harris and the 20th Century Club. Mom and Dad would play together and frequently invite a couple home with them for cocktail hour after the game. It was those times that I recall sitting in our library as they all sipped highballs and analyzed the day's hands at bridge. I usually sat on the floor, quietly playing solitaire. The grownups were nice to me but I stayed somewhat separate.

Looking back, it seems I just wanted to be near my mother. It feels like I was trying to protect her, staying close just in case. In case of what? I don't know. Maybe I just wanted to be there in case she would notice me, pay attention to me, spend time with me. It seemed there was never enough of that. Even now I am not sure if that impression is realistic or just reflects the insatiable childish desire for parental attention. Even the moments of recognition, like when I presented my report card for her signature, were never long enough. Our eyes would meet briefly and I would look for that approval but, even before we broke eye contact, she was already gone, her mind moving on to whatever was next or maybe just retreating inward.

I found a postcard to my sister one day. It was in our breakfast room, in the ceramic bowl that held the incoming mail after it spilled in through a slot in the front door and splattered across the floor until someone came along, picked it up and separated out the business mail to place it on the stairs to go up to Dad's office. I must have been eight or nine when I found the card. I doubt if I ever received much mail but for some reason my attention was drawn to the bowl. I don't recall the picture on the postcard, but on the back were words that confused me so much I went to my mother to ask what they meant. First she scolded me for reading other people's mail and then explained. As I remember it, the card was signed by Frank Washburn. It was addressed to my sister and told her that her father was innocent. Until that day, I had no idea that my sister's father was someone other than my own father. Learning in this way that my older brother and sister had a different father than I did was a major shock. I remember feeling very confused about getting scolded for reading something that was right out there in the mail bowl. If it was so damn private why didn't someone just give it to my sister? (Of course I didn't say anything because we all knew that the only one in the family who was allowed to get mad was mother.)

I felt set up by the circumstances, though I could not have named that at the time. I presume my mother told me that day about my Nana's murder. I remember being taken to Nana's grave at Fairmount Cemetery. But I have no recollection of putting together that this man in prison and my grandmother's death were connected. I was in the back seat of the car one day just after that when my mother asked my sister if she wanted to go to prison to visit her father. I remember my arms reaching over the front seat as I leaned in to listen more carefully. I said I wanted to go. I was ignored. I wonder if my sister was hurt. It all seems very vague, like a memory housed in water that swirls and swishes around, making the details not only unclear but constantly changing.

Over time I came to understand the crime, but I was given very few details. I do remember hearing about a piece of wire and testimony by the person who sold the wire to Washburn as being the undeniable evidence of his guilt. My mother never told me about her decision to marry Washburn. I wish I had understood that better as I was growing up. I suppose it was too painful and perhaps too shameful for her to share it with me.

At first barely perceptible, in that tangle of unexpressed feelings was the beginning of a tiny fissure in my world. What I had thought to be true about my family simply was not. The fissure widened into a crack, was on its way to becoming a gulf and then a chasm. If my family wasn't all that I had been made to believe, then what else about the security and predictability of my life was also rooted in falseness? Of course, it's obvious now that the card was a set-up. How difficult it must have been for her to figure out how to open the topic with her youngest child, something so close to unspeakable; such a long-term lie.

My mother was primarily a rancher. She ran our home with the help of several individuals including a wonderful woman named Bea Woods, who came every weekday afternoon to cook dinner for us. Bea provided an invaluable sense of continuity in my young life. She was a positive-minded woman with the strength of her spiritual beliefs to guide her life. She was a strong presence, an anchor even, in our home. I don't recall ever talking to Bea about my discovery of the truth about my family. But I imagine she knew about it. Everyone in town had read those newspaper articles I researched so many years later. I genuinely loved Bea and remember still how nice it was to hug her even though my arms couldn't go very far around. I am forever grateful for my mother's reminders after every meal to go and thank Bea for her efforts. Bea nurtured us, fed us in so many ways beyond the meals on the table.

On one of those warm West Texas summer evenings, Bea needed a ride home. Her husband usually picked her up, but I guess they were having car trouble or something. I was curious to see where she lived and I wanted to go along. We walked to my mother's car and I automatically made for the door to the back seat. I stopped suddenly though because, in some subtle way, my mother let me know that I was to sit in front with her. Now this made no sense to me at all. I was generally the polite, quiet child. The rules were that we respected adults and that meant they always sat in the front seat. I don't remember the rest of the drive. I think what is most painful about that memory is the probability that Bea noticed my confusion and saw me comply with my mother's subtle communication of the unstated rule. Bea had to witness my indoctrination into the world of Black and White. I had done nothing to earn the privilege in which I lived. But I had no awareness of that at the time. I complied with the unjust social convention in order to simply comply with my mother's wishes. I suppose this is how conventions become ingrained and engulf succeeding generations until mindful thought and action bring about change.

Not many years later, Bea was killed in a car crash, wearing no seat belt when a drunk ran a stop sign. That was probably the second funeral I attended. I remember the Baptist minister asking us all, "Are you ready?" The audience responded in a variety of ways - from non-verbal to very vocal. That service was a lot livelier than Emmanuel Episcopal Church! At some point all of the mourners were at Bea's house. I remember being so self-conscious, being the only white family in the home. One woman broke the ice with my mother and that made it better. I had been raised in a segregated world and hardly knew the other world existed until then. There was not a single child of color in my classroom at school. I was as uncomfortable around all those black folks as I had been comfortable with Bea one-on-one. One-on-one, of course, Bea was relating to me in *my* world, *my* culture. I didn't know how to relate in hers. It wasn't the people that made me uncomfortable; it was the understanding that my family had more - more of just about everything tangible - than so many other people. I was embarrassed by my privilege.

Although I never adopted the fundamental beliefs that support racism, I spent too many years estranged and isolated from any understanding of minorities in America and the financial discrepancies and power differentials that create and maintain racist attitudes. Even in college, when I finally received a more expanded sense of history in lectures by socialist historians about the Haymarket uprisings and by reading *Native Son*, I responded less with understanding and opening to these other worlds and more with an irresolvable white guilt. I even remember writing a paper about white guilt in a critique of Paul Schraeder's film, *Working Class*. The paper got an "A." Yet

I hadn't gained any real sense of ease about the other cultures in America. My guilt stood in the way until I was in my forties.

But, at that tender age, around nine or ten, when Bea had such a profound influence on my life, two other things took place that left a deep impression. I was sitting with my father watching TV when the news report showed film of a Buddhist monk in Vietnam who'd drenched himself in something flammable and struck a match in protest of the war in Vietnam. This black and white image highlighted the contrast between the dark sky and the bright flames as they rose up at an angle from his seated body – a crackling brilliance stabbing the blackness first here, then there, as it rode on the breeze into the flat nothing of the night sky. I still have a nearly kinesthetic sense of that image showing the flames carrying something sacred into the cosmos with hundreds gathered to witness the protest and the sacrifice. True martyrdom.

I don't know if it was before or after that TV horror that my mother told me about Gilbert, the gardener. He had died. She told me he had drenched himself in gasoline and lit himself on fire. I think she said it was because he had troubles with his wife. As an adult looking back on that, I struggled to understand why she would have thought it appropriate to share those details with me at my tender age. These were shocking introductions to the deeply disturbing notion that one might make an overt choice not to live life.

These events were all disturbing in themselves. The way they came together in the same time period definitely signaled the loss of my innocence. What had been a mostly idyllic childhood seemed to end all at once. (I did not yet have any recollection of the mistreatment I had experienced in Iran.) All of my material needs were met – and then some. I had enjoyed ten years of living life without many concerns at all. I know I had a lot more freedom from worry than many, many other children. And even though I felt it was lacking, I am also acutely aware that I had more emotional support than many children as well. I don't believe I ever spoke my feelings of sadness to anyone about all of these things. I don't think I had the words.

My brother, Jamie, was my best buddy. Well, at least when he wasn't my worst enemy. One day when he and I scuffled and argued over something, he hit me hard. It hurt and I was mad! I told on him and was upset when nothing happened to him, no punishment. It felt so unjust. The incident probably blew over but I remember considering suicide around that time. I was going to jump from my second story window onto the marble and brick terrace below. I recall wondering about the damage it would do to my body. I think I was still angry because my brother never seemed to get in trouble for being mean to me. Typical sibling rivalry, I suppose, but I know that not many kids think about doing themselves in at that age. I remember feeling like I just couldn't get my mother or my father to hear me or see me.

Mother was always in bed across the hall from my room before my bedtime. Instead of getting tucked in, I had a nightly ritual of watching TV in my parents' room, then going to kiss them both goodnight before I turned off my lights and crawled in to my bed. Only recently have I come to wonder if the sense of not being protected by my parents had its roots in Tehran. Perhaps it was simply the news of two suicide deaths - one a world away and the other very close to home - that caused my thinking to go in that direction. I began to feel invisible and only found the name for the feeling many years later. It took some years after that to begin to see invisibility as an attribute, not to be resisted or resented.

Whatever pain I was experiencing at that time blew over or re-submerged. I never attempted suicide. But things were changing in my family and soon my sister was sent away to boarding school. A year later, there was discussion about all of the children attending boarding school. My parents told us they wanted us to go away to boarding school to protect us from the animosity of the upcoming lawsuit over the condemnation of the ranch. The other reason - more likely the real reason - was that Mother's depressive illness was worsening and the psychiatrist saw the possibility of sparing all of us children the mental turmoil and other ill effects of living with a severely depressed mother.

I have no clear memory of mother's deteriorating mental health in those years. I saw her drinking alcohol daily but she was almost always with my dad and or their friends. So I just figured that was what adults do. I don't recall feeling rejected by the boarding school idea. I do remember saying goodbye to a girlfriend with whom friendship had recently become cemented. On the back staircase of our home, she told me how much she wanted me to stay there with her for the coming school year. I remember telling her that I felt I had to go because it was what my mother needed.

Even at age 11, I was tuned right in to my mother's needs. More than my own. There is the root of the "child of an alcoholic parent" pattern that I would work to reverse as an adult. I was willing, perhaps even eager, to comply with my parents' wishes in this and most other matters. It would have been too threatening to consciously entertain the thought that they were rejecting me. I remember thinking that boarding school would be kind of an adventure. Going would surely mean that I was grown up. But when I look back at my yearbook, I see the lack of commitment I had to boarding school. The little comments that classmates wrote each year are filled with references to hoping that I would be back the following year. I obviously was never sure where I would be and I suspect I was hoping for the possibility of being able to go home again, to have a normal family life; to go to school in the morning, come home at night and play with friends on the weekends. As strong as the pull was for me to be grown up, there was an equally strong desire in me to regress and return to that naïve youth before the ugly realities had been revealed to me.

I think I was already in high school when I saw my grade school sweetheart, David, again. We were at the airport at the end of Christmas vacation. I had become a hippie and there was David in his military academy uniform. Our eyes met and there was that spark of recognition. I remember judging him, wondering how he could identify himself with the military mindset. I judged him harshly but scarcely realized I was doing it. I looked away. I just didn't know what to say. Of course I realize now that he probably was not wearing that uniform by choice. That moment of connection haunts me some even now. I wish I had found words to say something, even just a greeting. This was the first boy I had really trusted, besides my brother.

A few years ago a dear childhood friend found the right time to tell me that David had already died at age thirty-something. His liver gave out after too many years of abusing alcohol. I was flooded with sadness at the life of missed opportunity punctuated by that fleeting opportunity the last time I had seen him in the incongruent intimacy of our small-town airport. I wonder if he was abusing alcohol before or after he went to the military academy. And how uncanny that I had such an attraction to him even in grade school – this boy who became an alcoholic like all those other alcoholics I tried to love until I got clean and sober myself and then began to discover more of who I am.

This pull that alcoholism in the family exerts on children is amazing and mysterious to me. When a parent is more involved with alcohol than with the family, some predictable personality traits emerge in the children. John Bradshaw's work in this area is well known now.

The first born is generally the Hero child, the outgoing, successful child who excels in school and extracurricular activities. This child creates or at least helps maintain the façade in the community that everything is just fine in the family. The second child, unable to compete with the success of the first, becomes the Scapegoat – the child who, by contrast, cannot do anything well, tends strongly toward poor judgment, academic troubles and even social difficulties. The third child becomes the Lost Child, the one that no one sees or hears. Without feedback from parents and others, children do not develop a sense of their own identity – their abilities, skills and talents – and often drift into adulthood shrouded in this veil of uncertainty. The fourth child is the Mascot. Unable to tolerate the undercurrent of tension in the family that often spills into the moment, the Mascot uses humor and playfulness to draw attention to self, deflecting attention away from the discord. [124]

I can see myself in my mascot role actually trying to accomplish the spiritual work mentioned previously – distracting my mother from her pain so that she could see a glimmer of hope long enough to grab hold of it. I think that was my spiritual quest long before I could name it as such. The fact that she did not respond to my efforts does not mean I did not succeed. I played out my role and learned from it – eventually. I also have some of the traits of the Lost Child – invisibility being a strong cue. I wonder if that is because I followed my brother, Jamie, into my teens. He was the reliable one to me.

All children raised in families where alcoholism is active, even if not yet evident to family members, are at greater risk for becoming alcoholics or marrying alcoholics. I fit so perfectly into the mode of Mascot that it is really a little scary. I would put money on my friend, David, being a second-born Scapegoat child. It is amazing to me that we were drawn to each other at such a young age. If we had grown up together, dated and eventually married, we would have been the perfect couple – an alcoholic man with a codependent wife. We would have danced that painful dance that adults get caught up in when one person tries to rescue another from alcoholism with painful chaos roaring up because the alcoholic does not want to be saved, but the codependent feels compelled to keep trying.

CHAPTER SEVEN

Lost

As long as we remained symbiotically linked, there was always
hope that it was not too late to get from her the perfect love we
always wanted. Now we are grown and we know we never will.
~Nancy Friday

I went away to boarding school near Phoenix, Arizona. I made friends easily and remember being happy, once I got through the initial homesickness. The kindest thing my sister ever did for me was to get permission for me to spend one night in her room in the high school dorm. Just being close to her seemed to heal the hurt and I was able to return to my dorm the next night feeling better. I finished sixth grade and was back to start seventh the following year. Because I had started school a year late, due to a November birthday, teachers determined that I really should be in eighth grade. So, halfway through the school year, I joined new friends in Mr. Stormont's classroom at Judson School in Scottsdale.

Overnight, I went from being one of the older kids in the class to one of the youngest. I don't think the academics phased me, but I was having trouble finding my way socially. By ninth grade, I was already beginning to get lost. Cigarettes had been familiar to me for several years. Then I tried pot for the first time. I remember an oh so mature upper classman, Nancy, inviting me and two others out into the desert with a tiny little roach, the stub end of a marijuana joint. This girl just exuded cool. She was tall with very long, silvery-blonde hair, parted in the middle. There was something about the way her hair and her part came down her forehead that gave her an air of aloofness and power. Plus, she was from Las Vegas – a paragon of cool, in my mind. So out we went, into the desert with one roach between four of us. We all got one or two hits and I remember pretending to be high even though I'd never seen anyone under the influence of pot. I so wanted to fit in. I don't actually recall the first time I was truly under the influence. But I found myself there more and more often as I progressed through high school.

At the end of ninth grade, after a visit with a friend in California, I flew back to Texas, but not San Angelo. My mother was in a private psychiatric hospital in Dallas and would be there for most of the summer. My father had leased a townhouse nearby and we would visit her at times throughout the summer. So I got lost in another way - in a strange town with no friends except my brother. There was a pool we used frequently and no one was watching my father's liquor cabinet.

I was struggling to find myself - as most teens are - when I decided on a school in northern Arizona that I wanted to try. It was an alternative school with different ideas about grades and restrictions. I didn't apply myself there much but managed to graduate anyway. I don't know how I would have navigated the public schools in my hometown but, at the same time, navigating those schools might have prepared me better for life in the real world. By the end of my senior year, I had gotten something of an education and had figured out how to cope with shyness by staying high on pot whenever possible throughout all four years. I had taken some journeys with other drugs as well and justified it all by believing the trips were helping me come to know myself more completely. At the very least, I learned how to maintain and appear normal even when my mind was in an altered state and my emotions were following suit.

I had two best friends who would include me in their explorations of the mountains surrounding the school. One day, in the late afternoon, we climbed the five hundred feet up the little mountain we all called "Napoleon." We crossed over its saddle and went to the left, out onto a ledge that is about a foot wide in my memory but probably was more like two. We sat there and smoked some pot, looking out over the beautiful red sandstone desert with clumps of green foliage. We were laughing about something. Marie had stood up and turned around to look up at the cliff face above us. That shifted her center of balance and she swayed backwards a little. I remember her arms turning like windmills to regain her balance when, in the unmistakable slow-motion of a marijuana high, Carrie reached out and curled her fingers into Marie's shirt to stabilize her and bring her back to us. It was about a sixty-foot drop onto a hard slab of sandstone. We have all three wondered how any of us survived our adolescence. We *know* that magical Verde Valley was protecting us.

When the end of high school came, I was relieved to be finished and made up my mind to do better in college. In all those years of high school, I heard little to nothing about Washburn. He had applied for parole many times, though. I know that my parents' attorney followed the situation and probably filed some responses to his parole requests. I was told that, from his prison cell, Washburn hounded my aunt with letters threatening her and the safety of her husband and children. I know of no such letters written to my mother. I wonder if Washburn held my aunt more responsible for his eventual prosecution. Maybe she did have something to do with the Houston police making such a large contribution to solving the crime. It certainly doesn't read that way – it looks like Detective Thompson just happened to have ears in the right place and the savvy to follow through on the information he gathered.

Due largely to the letters, Washburn was denied parole time after time. But, finally, sometime in the 1970s I think, he was set free. I was told he was sent to live in Arizona. My aunt told me much later that, at the time, Governor Dolph Briscoe called her personally to inform her of – and apologize for – Washburn's pending release. I later learned that Washburn had heart trouble. A lawyer I met years later told me convicts are often paroled when medical problems (that would be very expensive for the state to fix) begin to appear on the criminal's health horizon. It seems a little eerie that I had spent so much time in Arizona and this sociopath ended up there for the last years of his wasted life. But I know he was not there when I was graduating from high school in 1973. His request for parole that year was denied. He was still claiming that the search of his garage which turned up the bits of highly incriminating wire was illegal.

Only a few years ago, when I tracked down his death certificate, I was astonished to learn that he reportedly served in World War II and also that he was married after his parole. His death certificate listed his wife as the "informant" who provided facts of his identity and his death. Whether he was ever actually paroled to Arizona or not, I don't know. This could have been a little fib designed by my parents to allay the potential fears of my siblings and me. He died in Texas though, way up north, on New Year's Eve in 1979. He was 63. Cardiac arrest. I wonder if my mother knew.

Learning that he had been married softened my thoughts about him and confronted me with my continued need to heal the wound that this man – whom I had never met – had brought about in my soul. If I really believe that each of us enters into this world with contracts involving other souls who agree to bring us lessons in the form of conflicts, pain and even the lighter things in life, then I would have to thank Harry Washburn for his horrendous crime. In the spiritual context, he was willing to murder and spend 24 years incarcerated so that my mother would have the opportunity to take the journey of learning to forgive herself; so I could have the experience of losing and then finding my true nature and my soul's purpose.

CHAPTER EIGHT

Replication

We are all linked, one to another. We answer, though we have heard no voice. We respond, though we do not know we have been summoned. And the universe responds to us — with powers you could not think were there, by ways you had no forethought of, bringing help you could not know would come.
~James Dillet Freeman

Before I graduated from high school, my parents left San Angelo and moved to Austin. After graduation, I lived with them while I dallied for about six months and then started college with a determination for greater academic success. I missed the orientation sessions but started at the University of Texas in January. The campus was huge and I was both shy and introverted. Somehow I found my way around and worked fairly hard to make good grades. I shared my off-campus apartment with my live-in boyfriend, Rob, who slept all day and usually stayed up all night writing the short story that seemed to never get finished.

At some point, my last attempt to save Mother involved swimming laps in my parents' pool and getting her to swim with me. When I reflect back on how instrumental she was in my learning to swim, the role reversal is obvious. But I had no conscious awareness of that at the time. We simply had always enjoyed the water together. She was clearly alcoholic by then. Isolated and drinking earlier and earlier every day. Too shy to find myself in that huge student body, perhaps the time spent with her was a convenient distraction from my own loneliness. I just so much wanted her to be something more, to do something more rewarding with her life - all the things a parent would want for her child and all of them a projection of my own developmental struggle at the time. I had not yet found a foundation for the life of purpose that I was meant to live.

I believe I had already started college when I asked my father one day, somewhat angrily and in a very demanding way, "What's wrong with her?!" He was patient and slow to reply that she was depressed and addicted to alcohol and, likely, somewhat brain-damaged from drinking so much and perhaps from the many series of electroconvulsive therapy (ECT) treatments she had undergone (before ECT was reportedly improved to avoid causing brain damage.) I remember being horrified at my father's passivity. I felt he should have been doing something to prevent this misery. I knew so little then about the futility of trying to fix people who do not have it in them to fix themselves.

Something brought my mother's psychiatrist from Dallas to our home in Austin to visit. I don't know if this was in response to my question but I doubt if it was purely social. I recall a very brief conversation with him. It was the only time I had ever discussed my own feelings on the topic of Washburn with anyone. I shared my understanding that mother had brought this misery on herself with her choice to marry Washburn to begin with. The doctor insisted that Mother had little choice in whom to marry, reviewing the pressures to marry that were placed on her by her mother and stepfather. If that meeting with the doctor was meant to be our family therapy, it certainly was brief and inconclusive. I doubt if I was the only child who wondered what was going wrong in our family. I was angry, though, that my mother could just throw her life away. More role reversal. I judged my mother harshly, in ways I would come to deeply regret.

I didn't understand then that judgment is always a projection. We see in the other something we dislike about ourselves and then, in our efforts to deny that thing's existence within ourselves, we condemn the other for having the very trait. I was projecting outward my deep confusion about the risks involved in making such important decisions as whom to love and how to know when it is right to marry. A self-actualized person will see that the judgment projected onto others is always a crystal clear mirror for us to confront ourselves and grow toward greater self-acceptance.

Family therapy, as I studied it in graduate school, had its beginnings in the mid-1950s. It must have evolved considerably by the 1970s. If her psychiatrists ever recommended therapy for all of us, Mother never pursued it and we were left to figure things out on our own. Or maybe my parents simply relied on doctors to address these concerns and had no knowledge of the benefit that a therapist could provide. I wonder if my mother's horrific experience with the social workers in family services during her divorce left her reluctant to pursue that level of expertise. Without any insight into the family dynamics and my role in them, many years would pass before I learned of the pitfalls of being the child of an alcoholic, taking on the parental role and learning to be a rescuer with a high probability of becoming an alcoholic myself or marrying one.

So I went to university classes every day with 40,000 other students and managed to make that work for me. I met my third best friend by the pool one day in early spring. I had noticed her and her husband with their little girl. My friend was pale-skinned with dark curly hair; very Irish. She had left the Emerald Isle for warmer climes in Africa and married a Nigerian academic, a man with Yoruba roots. Their daughter, Iyabo, was the most precious child I had ever known. With beautiful black eyes, cocoa skin and a smile that could have calmed a torrent, she was four at the time. We had a wonderful friendship for about two years and then they had to leave. The boxes were packed and back they went to Nigeria. Correspondence was frequent at first, but I soon realized I had all but lost my only friend from college so far. I also felt I had lost myself again and was trying to find some meaning in my academic choices.

(Many years later I found her again, living in London after she was suddenly deported from Nigeria for purely political reasons. They put her on a plane in her tropical African dress and sent her to London in mid-winter with only her passport and whatever money she'd had in her purse at the time. I doubt it was her politics that caused this; more likely the social and political upheavals that continued to plague Nigeria's entrance into the 20th century world economy. Still, London in winter, in a T-shirt and a sarong?)

I was half way through college. I had no academic goals and nothing that was pulling me toward a career. I didn't know myself well enough to know what I wanted for my life. My father was aware of how well I had done in my studies of languages: Spanish in high school and French more recently. He suggested I spend a year in France. I was reluctant and felt it would be too expensive. I remember my father's attitude was along the lines of "spend the money now because it may not be available forever." That seemed rather foreboding, but I was convinced that going would be a good thing. Looking back, I see clearly that I was running from my emptiness, trying to find meaning in the potential that was out there, overseas, somewhere. As I ran from myself, I created a certainty in my dream of France. The plans gave me focus and I emerged from my doldrums. I spent the summer in Paris in an intense course of advanced language and culture training. The teacher was a socialist and gave an interesting perspective on European history. The city was amazing but lonely for me. John, a friend that my brother and I had grown up with, came over to study as well. He missed his boyfriend so much that, after a few weeks, he returned to New York to live. Just over ten years later he would be dead from AIDS, even though, as he put it, he never had any of those wild nights out on Fire Island.

By autumn I had tired of the interminable press of life in the big city. Crowds of people everywhere and such expenditure of energy just to live daily life! I considered returning home but a couple of phone calls and a letter from my father convinced me to stay. The academic years were out of sync so I would have been returning in October with no plans of how to use my time until the spring semester in the U.S. began in January.

Much like my own mother at that age, I was drifting. It was my great good fortune that, unlike my mother's experience, it was not my parents' plan to find a mate for me and encourage or force me into a marriage that held no promise. That said, I do recall my mother trying to set me up with her hairdresser, a man at least ten years older than I was and not at all educated. She did not pressure me in the slightest but, still, what a strange resemblance this bears to her introduction to Washburn. Both were men with less education, perhaps less intelligence and probably less potential for success than the woman. Perhaps a mother just wants to see her daughter settled. Career or husband – pick one so life can truly begin. On the other hand, some things are transmitted from one generation to the next, simply because they never quite come to conscious awareness. Just like my family's unexamined attitude toward black people. Overall, though, I think my mother chose to raise her children differently than her mother had raised her. As passive as she was in her parenting, there were many choices my mother made that honored the individual that I was. It was probably painful for her to see me drifting. I like to think she had faith in me to eventually find what I was seeking in life.

In France in September, craving a calmer and warmer atmosphere, I went south and found a program in Montpellier that suited me perfectly. The climate was gentle and the people more open. The train ride took me down the central valley of France, through the town of Arles where Van Gogh's *Bedroom at Arles* floated into my head: its bright yellows against vibrant blues and the few accoutrements of simple living placed casually around the room. I arrived at Montpellier to find the buses were on strike. I walked forever to get to the campus. I enrolled, found lodging near a bus line – hoping the strike would be brief – and settled in to the adventures and the routines of the French academic year from October to June.

I met a number of non-French students, mostly Americans, and made some friends. But with the inevitable shortening of the days in the Fall came a slow descent into a mild depression. I felt the familiar fatigue and a return of the vague dissatisfaction with life that I attributed to not having a goal or purpose for my life. I was still lost and was really feeling it. I drank alcohol sometimes and smoked cigarettes in cafes with friends. We all walked and rode bikes through rain-soaked streets to get to cold classrooms where we sat, damp and chilled, day after day. As the weather got colder, I was swimming in the evenings for exercise and ended up with an ear infection. I was not certain how to get to a doctor and had very little money to pay him, so I stalled and put up with the headache until my eardrum burst one night and then would not heal. I got on a bus and got to a doctor who told me, "Vous avez un trou dans l'oreille." A hole in my eardrum. He suggested I wait to return to the U.S. to have it surgically repaired.

So I pursued my ability to communicate in French with a 95% loss of hearing in my left ear. Fortunately, the French are highly expressive in non-verbal ways and the language itself is formulated mostly at the front of the mouth. So I was able to rely partly on lip reading. It was also fortuitous that I had relocated to an area of the country where the local accent put emphasis on final syllables which otherwise—in Paris, especially - are so subtle that they are barely audible.

In early February, I started to come back out of the depression - right on schedule for seasonal affective disorder (SAD) - though I had no idea that was going on at the time. We studied and rode bikes to the beach on the weekends. I set aside funds and spent four days and three nights in Florence, Italy. We immersed ourselves in museums all day and danced at discos all night. On the train back to Montpellier, we were too tired to sleep and basically punch drunk, laughing and goofy, then finally sleeping like the dead for the last several hours. We were able to adjust all of the seats in the compartment to make one large flat surface. As we slept into the morning hours, the regular commuters got on the train and then found the conductor who rousted us for taking up too many seats. So we made room for the French with our rumpled clothes, unbrushed hair and bad breath. Only with the energy of youth can two weeks' worth of fun be packed into four days!

In the spring, my parents came to visit. My father had made arrangements for them to travel across the Atlantic as passengers on a freighter. It made for a very rough but also very adventurous crossing. It is a strange way to measure a mother's love, but I don't know that she would have agreed to the trip if I hadn't been at the other end of it. I met them in Rotterdam. I had been to Amsterdam just days before and had fallen in love with the Rijksmuseum where so many of Van Gogh's amazing paintings hung at that time. With little effort, I convinced them to go back there with me to enjoy the city and its treats. At the time I noticed no hesitation whatsoever on their part. I realized my mother was not in her prime - she seemed tired and not entirely well. When we arrived in Amsterdam and got checked in to the hotel, my mother never left. She sat in her room and drank her Bourbon and smoked cigarettes. I remember her like a sculpture, immobile except for the movement of her arm as she raised a glass or a cigarette to her lips, with thick curls of smoke suspended in the air above her and shafts of sunlight slicing through them. I was very concerned. I had not seen her in almost a year and she seemed to be only a shaving of the person I had known. Ever passive, she was drifting away from me, my father and, it seemed, from life itself.

My father convinced me not to worry. He, himself, had become accustomed to going on with his life regardless of her emotional state. To wait for her to feel better in order to continue to live his own life - our own lives - would have meant waiting forever. She simply wasn't traveling in that direction. So my father went with me out into the city with its many bridges and blonde people on bikes with big wheels. It was early, early spring and there were not yet signs of life renewing. It was rainy and cold outdoors but Vincent Van Gogh's art exuded warmth, vitality and wondrous visions of creation. There may even have been hope in the madman's paintings. Or perhaps that was just my projection. It had been said that Van Gogh ate the paint off his brushes and the metals made him crazy. Now the label of bipolar disorder or, more likely, temporal lobe epilepsy is offered to explain the creativity of his madness. I wonder by what apparent accident it was that I fell in love with a painter who may have suffered similar mental states as my mother. It was a couple of years later that I came to understand the cycles of my mother's emotional state and first heard of the diagnosis: "bipolar disorder."

Many years after my time in that great city, when I learned of the fearful and painful aspects of my mother's first stay in Amsterdam, gasping tears lurched from my heart. I was so very sad and remorseful that my silly enthusiasm may have required her to re-face what had been for her a prison-city, a dark night of her soul. I was so angry that neither parent had told me of the anguish they had endured in that city. How awful it must have been for her to remember her mental breakdown there. Years later, when I asked my father about this, he assured me that she likely didn't even remember her original stay in Amsterdam. The shock therapy in Tehran would have obliterated her ability to recall it. But I have to wonder where memories go when we no longer recall them. I felt in the depths of myself that she *had* remembered, that even if her conscious memory could not recall that time, she knew on some level where she was and how it had been for her those many years before. Perhaps, like a pre-verbal child, the memory was stored kinesthetically and she acted out the drama once again by confining herself to her room with her self-medication. For that suffering, *I* felt horribly responsible.

I learned of my mother's breakdown in Amsterdam when I was in my late thirties, during my time in graduate school. I had completed eighteen months of therapy to address my pattern of episodic depression. I then continued my healing by becoming trained as a counselor. It was already too late for me to alleviate my guilt directly, to make it better by going to my mother with an apology and a conversation with a hug at the end. There was no going to my father for absolution either. He did not see or hold that any harm had been done. So I was left with my guilt and my heartache to process in therapy. In countless prayers and private conversations with her in my head – and across the veil – I eventually was able to own only my part in the Amsterdam decision and to see that each of my parents had a part too. I came to forgive myself for not knowing what I did not know at the time. Separating my actual personal responsibility from my tendency to blame myself was the most difficult task. I learned to release that slicing self-condemnation by relying on my foundation of spiritual beliefs and the power of forgiveness which I learned to extend not only to my parents but to myself as well.

After the vacation with my parents, I was back at school in Montpellier. One of my American friends introduced me to a tall blonde Frenchman, very unlike the stereotype. He had a wonderful laugh and an outrageous handlebar moustache. He was studying to be a commercial airline pilot. He and two or three friends were hanging out with my girlfriend and we all spent some time together one evening. There was an undeniable attraction between Monsieur Moustaches and me – it was evident even without language. I think we had made arrangements to go out on an official date soon. He and his friends were out flying a few days later – fooling around, flying upside down – when they flew into a mountain. They must have died on impact. I didn't even know his last name or where he was from. I had no knowledge of a funeral or memorial. I talked to his friend – the only one that wasn't flying with them that day – who told me not to feel sad. I think he was trying to convince himself. I *did* feel sad. And, though I couldn't have named the feeling at the time, I also felt terribly abandoned. As uncomfortable as that was, I knew even then that this sense of being left alone was familiar. I was on my own again with the promise of something wonderful at the end of that long, lonely winter snatched right out of my hands. There was no closure. I didn't really allow myself to feel the grief I needed to feel. I simply didn't know how. It was too big a task for me to face all alone. So I ignored the feelings, shoved them down deep and made it through the end of the year.

I remember a story told by the amazing poet, David Whyte, at a reading in Grass Valley, California. He talked about Robert Bly's metaphor of the black bag that we all carry with us. The bag starts out small but, as we move through life, all of the things we don't want to face, feel or acknowledge go into the bag. David Whyte chuckled as he added a little Doppler effect - the sound that something like my grief for the Frenchman would make when I put it in that bag so fast I didn't even have to look at it - like a fast train passing by with the sound warped a bit. That is what it felt like for me. I just put it out of my mind. Over time, I fooled myself into believing this meant it was resolved.

It was May by then. I was ready to go home. The school year ended in June. I packed up and left. With a relief that felt like it lifted my feet from the ground, I put in action another geographical solution to my problems.

Returning to Texas was like culture shock all over again. My father picked me up at the airport in Austin and we drove in past "The University." A brand new pedestrian overpass on the northern edge of campus spanned six lanes of traffic. It was large and polished and looked very expensive. The relative opulence of this campus, as compared to the one I had just left where they waited arbitrarily until the first day of November to turn on the heat, was striking and other-worldly. That pedestrian overpass became an icon of opulence to me, a symbol of the indulgent American way. Even the English language seemed foreign to me. I remember a female voice on the car radio in a pronounced Texas accent. My judgment was that this person had to be completely ignorant, yet there she was being interviewed on the radio. There was something incongruent about it all. Then I realized the person speaking was Lady Bird Johnson. Whatever one's politics may be, this was an erudite woman. That radio show - as well as my very own country - seemed surreal to me.

Just before the last right turn to our home, I opened my little black bag long enough to tell my father about the wonderful Frenchman - how nice he had been and how funny. We stopped at a Stop sign and I said, "He died." My father, though, had turned away from me to look left for traffic. When he turned back and saw me waiting for his reaction, he just kind of smiled. The smile was so weird in the context of what I had just revealed. I couldn't make sense of it. I am certain now that he simply had not heard me. But I didn't realize that at the time. I didn't realize that there might have been a better time to bring up the topic. So, rather than asking him for a response that made sense, I interpreted his vacant look as some kind of appropriate response to the news of my broken heart.

It shocks me now that I simply accepted his incongruent smile without question. How accustomed had I already become to feeling invisible in my family? I didn't realize there was something very wrong with that exchange of communication. I was left with my grief and no guidance on how to weather it. I hadn't been home for more than an hour when my geographical solution began to fail. Back to the black bag with that piece of information! Some time went by and, several years later, I realized I could not even remember the name of that jovial Frenchman I had once wanted to love. I just buried the whole matter until years later when the memory resurfaced during graduate school.

That day in the car with my father marked another level of transition in my life from a childlike dependence on him to the realization and acceptance that there were some things I could no longer take to him with an expectation that he could make them better. He had telegraphed this in the letter he sent me in September of 1976 when I was in France debating whether to stay for the academic year or to return to Texas. Receiving this letter from my father was like the sort of frank conversation that a parent has with a child at the kitchen table when important life decisions are pondered.

For my father, education was the path to freedom and I understand now how distressing it was for him to see me flailing in the face of academic choices. The letter made me realize, finally, that he could not make my decisions for me, as he had throughout my childhood. Of course, I didn't know at the time that I was moving through a necessary developmental milestone on the way to maturity. I had not yet come to terms with the reality that I could not save my mother. Yet here was my father being quite clear that he couldn't save me from living my own life and facing the consequences of my own decisions. I think this stands out in my memory because many of the smaller conversations where I might have learned this from my parents did not take place because I was away at school. Without guidance from a steady and consistent caregiver, I was left to my own devices to figure out where I ended and others began, where my responsibility for myself started and others' responsibility for me ceased, where my dreams might one day meet reality.

A few days after my return, my father told me that my old boyfriend, Rob, had come to see him one night, late. When Dad said that Rob had asked him for money, my eyes met Dad's briefly and must have shown the wave of panic that swept through me. Just the asking was a little too close to Washburn's type of extortion. Something inside of me shut down in that moment and I couldn't have told you what it was. It also caused me to remember a time when I was in high school and my mother introduced me to a 26 year-old man named, ironically, Con. I kid you not. Mother had met him at a bar and the fact that she was introducing me to him carried a tacit approval of the possibility of us becoming a couple. Really? I think I was 15 or maybe 16. Then, later on, when I was 23 or so, she introduced me to her hairdresser, also as a possible boyfriend.

I declined to be involved with the two men my mother chose. All three of these events suggest a sense of fate or, more likely, the pattern of multigenerational unconscious acting out. Just as my mother's first husband had attempted to live off her parents' wealth, my boyfriend came begging to my father. Just as mother's parents had set her up in a marriage that suited them, so my mother tried to find me a partner. I presume she had no idea that her action was a replication of the way her parents set her up in such a disastrous marriage. Maybe she was trying to scare me. I think it is more likely that she was operating from unconscious patterning, deeply ingrained.

Most of us parent our children by copying the ways we were parented. Until we look at those patterns from a mature adult perspective and consciously choose to accept or change them, they can simply run our behavior without our paying attention. It is the only explanation that makes sense to me to explain why a woman whose life had been so disrupted by the manipulative interventions of her parents would take similar actions with her daughter. Unconscious replication. She may have just wanted me to be settled into a marriage, so she could have a sense that my life was on track and that I was now grown up, so that her role in raising me could be considered complete. I will never know for sure. Even still, her needs for me were apparently more important than allowing me to find my own way.

I think it was a couple of years later, in the spring of 1978, when mother descended into another very deep depression. She was probably talking to my father about killing herself. Something, at least, caused my father to believe that she needed to be in the hospital. But Mother refused to go. My father had insisted years before that she be admitted. That led to her three (or so) months at Timberlawn Hospital in Dallas in 1970. After that stay, she had made him promise to never again cause her to be admitted against her will. My father kept his promise and my mother plunged further into depression.

Then Marian arrived from San Angelo with her deep concern and caring that came from many years of friendship. My mother's long-time friend was able to convince her to enter the hospital one more time. I was probably twenty-three and probably had just heard the words "bipolar disorder" applied to my mother's condition.

I visited her at the hospital in Galveston and was allowed to stay in her room overnight. (This is a bizarre accommodation that would never happen in today's hospitals.) She didn't really seem to know why she was there and a nurse took me aside to let me know it would be better for her if I didn't remind her of circumstances that led to her stay. She had received yet another round of ECT treatments and was blissfully relieved of many of the memories that were causing her distress. Her depression eventually improved and she was released.

It may have been just after that when she and my father stayed for several weeks at a facility in the Texas Hill Country that, in retrospect, must have been an alcohol rehabilitation center. I believe I visited them there but the memory is very hazy. I do know they were advised to continue attending AA meetings after leaving the facility.

Alcoholics Anonymous was not talked about much until the later 1980s. But, thanks to several generations of people getting clean and sober, it is much better known now and still the most reliable way to remedy the spiritual bankruptcy that is alcoholism. As far as I know, this was the first time that Mother's reliance on alcohol had been made part of her medical/psychiatric treatment. After the stay in rehab, I don't think she ever attended another AA meeting. That is in keeping with the person she was – very proud. I can't imagine her ever going into such a meeting and being able to find even one thing in common with another soul there.

When I refer my own clients to AA, I always encourage them to look for the similarities rather than focusing on the differences. The differences abound. They separate us as human beings. The similarities, though, make us humble and ultimately much better candidates for successful recovery.

My parents' stay in the Hill Country immediately preceded my graduation from the University of Texas with my B.S. in Radio-TV-Film. It turned out that I would work on only two major films – *Raggedy Man* and *Blood Simple* – before throwing away a career in media because I felt I didn't fit in. That day, though, with my friends Jake and Caryn, I walked across the stage at the LBJ School of Public Affairs auditorium. My father was in the audience; I wondered if I had done him proud. Mother was at home in her chair with her bourbon nearby.

After four years, my emotional support system came down to these two friends from college. My father had given all that he knew how to give. My mother was simply unable to give that which she did not possess in herself. This is not to say that my mother gave me nothing. She taught me to swim, she taught me to love the land and to find beauty in storm clouds - a metaphorical wisdom I wish she could have applied to her own life. She also gave me insight into mental health and mental illness that I never would have found without the experience of being her daughter, though it took me many years to gather and absorb this. The gifts she gave me caused me to search more deeply for myself, for my own sense of the meaning and purpose of life. It was in my struggle to come to terms with her emotional absence from my life that I discovered who I am. The gifts she gave me, though, did not come in the form or in the order that I might have expected.

Mental illness, just like mental health, crosses over all the boundary lines of financial status, intelligence, physical abilities and resourcefulness. In the higher economic realms, mental illness is often easier to cope with because the disruption to a person's ability to work and otherwise function is not felt as acutely. Perhaps the one aspect of a cure for depression that does cross over these lines is the human need for a sense of belonging and meaning or purpose to our lives. That usually entails a relationship with something larger than ourselves, a quest that helps us ask and answer the existential questions – who we are and why we are here. Some people find their answers in physics. Others, like me, have found our answers in metaphysics and the exploration of different faith traditions.

My mother had once found a sense of purpose in managing the land she had inherited. When much of that was taken by the government to establish a useless lake, she did not explore a new way of being who she was – she didn't make the effort to "reinvent" herself. Perhaps she over-identified with what she did, with being a rancher. Then, absent any other identity, she *became* her illness. She was a depressed woman, a bi-polar woman, an alcoholic woman. She became her victim story – victimized first by her ex-husband and then by governmental action that deprived her of land that her ancestors had claimed, worked and lived off of for so many years. She was not just someone with an illness from which she could heal in time. She may have started out that way, but, I believe she never came to fully know and master the tools for personal change that she really needed in order to heal herself. She was traumatized, to be sure, by the sociopath she had been forced to marry, but she was not responsible for his actions.

She was the victim of his crime as much as her mother was. But her mother, Nana, was not a victim. Even when Washburn confronted her and Papa and the ranch, forcing her to write a fake suicide note, Nana maintained the capacity to intelligently craft the letter with grammatical errors that would cause anyone to realize Papa had not written it. In that way, Nana stayed in her power even while Washburn tried to make victims of them both. For my mother to have moved out of victim, she would have had to find within herself the ability to lift off the heavy weight of guilt and to put an end to her suffering through recurring stabs of culpability that she felt for her mother's murder. She bought in to her own victim story and it destroyed her.

Forgiveness of self is the first order of business in healing mental health concerns. Not one of us is perfect and yet we often hold ourselves up to higher standards than anyone else. We berate ourselves for our choices that have not worked out well and, in the process, forget that we did not know what we did not know when we first made the choice. We rage against parents who did or didn't do or be one thing or another. We project our disappointments in ourselves onto those around us and the misery self-perpetuates – until we stop it by stepping out of its path and letting go of the self-judgment that would keep us stuck in the perpetual motion of this vicious cycle.

In forgiving others, we sometimes get stuck in a different place because we think that forgiving is synonymous with pardoning or condoning their misbehavior. Forgiving is neither pardoning nor condoning. Forgiveness is a process from which we make the choice to return to feeling predominantly peaceful within ourselves even though something bad – even horrible – has happened to or around us. Forgiveness is this conscious choice to feel at peace even when we have been wronged. The power of this is most evident in situations where justice cannot be found through the court systems. Consider the specter of the perpetrator of some unspeakable crime dying before he is accused and brought to court or one who is never caught. Victims in these situations must find a way to release feelings of hatred and desire for retribution if they are to overcome the victimization and proceed to thrive in life. The motivation to achieve and experience inner peace has to be stronger than the inertia that would hold a person in resentment. The key point is that either one of these destinations is a choice. The choice for peace starts with a thought: I let go.

The process of letting go seems insurmountable at first when it involves another person and can be equally daunting when we are faced with forgiving ourselves. Yet with the moment-to-moment discipline of returning our thoughts to peace and serenity within comes the healing of our broken places. How many times have you heard someone say they would not have wished their terrible experience on their worst enemy, but now that they have found their way through it, they are grateful for the experience? This is how we come to live life instead of allowing life to live us. We do well to rise up to whatever is before us.

I am convinced that the thing my mother could not do was to forgive herself for knowing and then marrying the man that eventually murdered her own mother. The only mistake she made was deciding to marry him. That did not leave her responsible for his actions. Yet she obviously suffered over the event long after it took place. Perhaps the effects of bipolar disorder caused her to inevitably return to this suffering. It seems obvious that she lived with low self-esteem for reasons not entirely clear to me. Or perhaps she descended into it with the onset of her alcoholism.

She was the second born in her own alcoholic family system. As mentioned previously, Scapegoat is the title for the family role she filled.[125] She filled it well. She probably never felt her efforts were quite up to par. Other perceptions of herself as wrong or bad probably just piled on top of that, building an increasingly damaged self-concept that perpetuated her depression.

Perhaps in protection of my half-siblings and probably out of some degree of shame, she could not really share her feelings about the crime perpetrated on her mother by the father of her first two children. It was never talked about openly in our family. She likely shared her feelings with her new husband, my father, over and over again. She certainly shared them with a series of psychiatrists. It seems any feelings that might have leaked out elsewhere were denied or stuffed inside or shut off with alcohol and a variety of prescription drugs. Wounds without air will fester instead of heal. Secrets held in dark hearts do the same.

My mother must have had manic episodes during my youth but I was sheltered from them, sent away to school as she wrestled with the mood swings. Even in our summers as a family, I never saw what I would now recognize as mania. What I *did* see was the depression. Later on, in my twenties, as she was entering menopause, I witnessed her one time in the throes of mania. I was poorly equipped to respond with any compassion or understanding. For the first time in my life, I heard her outlandish claims. In her own eyes, she was an athlete, preparing for the Olympics. She said so one day on the phone with her lawyer. I was on the phone as well, trying to help her with some detail. I was embarrassed that her disorder was so evident now to people who had once really admired her. After the call, she fell in a parking lot as she was demonstrating her expansive athletic ability and prowess.

I was confused and was just beginning to understand the effects of bipolar disorder. Not long after that fall, she began to sink again. I didn't know it at the time. I was busy in my work managing a nightclub. It amused me, kept me out late and justified the occupational hazard of my cocaine habit.

CHAPTER NINE

Memorial

Do not stand at my grave and weep. I am not
there, I do not sleep. I am a thousand winds that blow.
I am the diamond glints on snow. I am the sunlight
on ripened grain. I am the gentle autumn rain.
~Mary Elizabeth Frye

On Memorial Day of 1981, just after noon, I woke up to a phone call from my father who sounded a little tense. The fog in my head was beginning to clear a bit when I heard him say that my mother was dead. It made no sense to me - she had not been sick, even though she wasn't exactly well either. "How?" is what I asked in a confused and sleepy voice. She had shot herself.

I dressed quickly and still remember exactly what I was wearing: a V-neck T-shirt with narrow, multicolored stripes and a pair of jean shorts with very small pockets on the thigh over the side seam. The pocket flaps were round and a metal button held them closed. I didn't leave my home in those days without a small vial in one of those pockets. I drove the ten minutes to my parents' home and was in the living room, around the corner from the staircase, when I heard the paramedics bringing the gurney down, struggling a bit to navigate the ninety degree turn in the stairs. The two men spoke with my father briefly and I remember one of them was about my age and quite nice-looking. He looked directly at me with the glare from the picture window all around him. I imagine his eyes held a great deal of compassion but I couldn't meet his gaze. I lowered my eyes, feeling very self-conscious. Then they were gone.

My father and I sat in the large stuffed chairs in the living room directly below the bathroom where she had shot herself. That living room ceiling had always seemed a little low but it took on a truly oppressive feeling that day – as though the weight of the tragedy that unfolded on the other side of it was measurably bearing down on the space we occupied. Not much time went by before the room darkened down slightly in the mid-afternoon. Cloud cover had rolled in. Then the sky just opened up, delivering a ferocious amount of rain. The drops were practically horizontal and the kitchen window began leaking as it never had before. My father made some phone calls. Time seemed to stand still as I watched the curtains of water move across the view from that kitchen window. When my parents' friend, Jack, came by, he told us he had taken a different route because of flash flooding. He stayed for a while and little was said. He was in shock just like the two of us. We were trying to reach my siblings; only one lived locally. Jack was kind and supportive and, after a while, he left.

Finally we reached my sister. She came with her young daughter and was helpful in calling a man to come get the blood-soaked carpet out of the bathroom. I imagine he used a carpet knife to cut out the first small section of shag carpet from the bathroom floor. I watched him carry out that first section through the hallway as it dripped red blood from what had been a white and gold carpet. Wanting to protect the hallway carpet, I got trash bags for the rest and helped him contain the mess. I think I also wanted to hide the blood, hide what had happened, but I was not conscious of that motivation at the time. He carried a couple of bags to the dumpster outside, where the college student/residents of the complex could have been walking by. I was surprised at how much blood there was. I learned later that my mother had used the .22 caliber pistol to shoot herself in the right temple. There was no exit wound. She had basically bled to death on the floor of her bathroom. (In her open casket, everyone could see the tiny flap of skin that covered the entry wound.)

Once the carpet was gone, there was some wiping up to do. It never occurred to me that, perhaps, that was not my job. I was there and it needed to be done, so I just got started. I remember thinking as I rinsed the sponge in her bathroom sink, that this would be how my healing process would begin. It was an odd thought for me because I had never really thought about healing before. It was as if some deep part of me knew that this grief would be the wave to carry me into my life.

I rinsed and I rinsed. It felt like one last way I could try to take care of her. Behind me, in the shower stall, I found the crimson colored nightgown they had cut off of her as they tried to save her. There also was a short strip of paper with jagged lines that showed the last beats of a heart as measured by the EKG. I saved that piece of paper for many years, hidden away in a journal whose whereabouts was always very clear to me though I wrote in it rarely. That paper strip became part of a ritual for me. I would take it out, look at it and feel the numbness that stayed with me long after I quit using cocaine. I knew each time that I was not yet over her death. Even now, I don't know if the paper registered my mother's heartbeats, or if it was a record of the paramedics' previous call. I don't suppose it ever really mattered.

My father and I drank Scotch together that afternoon and made more phone calls. The alcohol in the middle of the day just seemed like the thing to do. I didn't yet know that I would struggle to remove alcohol from my lifestyle before it *became* my life, as it had become my mother's.

The 1981 Memorial Day Floods in Austin were devastating to many. The Whole Foods Market, now a national chain, was establishing itself on Lamar Boulevard at the edges of downtown Austin about 150 yards from Shoal Creek. Right next to that creek stood a small house that was in the process of becoming an Italian restaurant. I had shopped at Whole Foods but knew nothing of the restaurant. Both of those establishments were flooded that weekend. The house had water marks about five feet up on the walls and the foundation of the house was at least twelve feet above the normal water level of the creek. Shoal Creek provided drainage for a huge portion of the city of Austin. The Whole Foods Market was also inundated. For many years after, sandbags would appear near its doors any time slightly more than light rain was predicted.

The day my mother died, I had been sleeping at noon when my father called because my work kept me out into early morning hours. My parents had invested in a nightclub that was doing very poorly. They asked for my help and I was struggling to turn it around. I had no particular training in running a business, but figured I could do better than the previous manager who never could seem to get proceeds to the bank. When mother died, we made the decision to cut our losses and shut the place down. So, as I was grieving the loss of my mother, I also faced what felt to me like my own business failure. Even though I had never really advocated for the opening of the business, I took its failure very personally.

There were many details to tend to. In addition to a broken lease and contracts to cancel, I had some equipment to sell for as much as I could to offset the losses. A man called to say he wanted the Perlick cooler I had for sale. He needed it, he said, because his cooler had been destroyed in the flooding of that house near the creek that he and his partner were renovating. How bizarre that the flood that punctuated my life's biggest tragedy was now connecting me to this charismatic man – Mr. Perlick Cooler. I sold him the cooler and by the end of that year was falling in love with him.

Falling in love was a wonderful distraction from the work of grieving. I managed to pretty much completely avoid feeling the feelings of loss, rejection, abandonment and anger that were roiling deep inside of me. Alcohol, pot and cocaine were my best friends and we hung out together a lot. I shared in a lifestyle of late nights, parties and hangovers as Mr. Perlick and I went through the motions of creating a life together. We bought a house and moved in. When

I wasn't working, I was caring for our home and, in my way, trying to be an adult when I had no clear picture of what that meant.

The substances that I used to numb my feelings also created the disinhibition that caused the pent-up grief to spill out when I was too messed up to make any sense of it. The tears would come and my mate would get frustrated with me, feeling the need to fix it all for me I guess. I saw a psychiatrist who correctly assessed delayed grief and told me to go to my mother's grave to say goodbye. I had always heard the phrase, "Time heals all wounds." I didn't know I had to actively do anything during the passage of all that time to get better.

Off I went to her graveside in San Angelo. I stayed a while and talked to her some. I was smoking a joint when the groundskeeper came near and seemed to linger for too long. I allowed him to chase me off. So I had hurried through the process in an altered state so that little, if any, healing really came of it. At any rate, the doctor didn't tell me that saying goodbye is a process, not an event. And letting go of a loved one who was really only partly there to begin with is that much harder when we also have to grieve the loss of hope for ever having the relationship that we thought was meant to be.

I continued to keep my psychiatric appointments and took anti-depressant medications, much like my mother had. I didn't tell my doctor I was still using cocaine, though I might have mentioned the pot. I continued through my life, carefully staying out of touch with my senses, feeling adrift, depressed, probably much like my mother had.

I didn't know then that staying out of touch with my senses was exactly what was keeping me stuck in that place of grieving. I now know that I needed to feel all of the feelings associated with the loss before I would be able to move on. It *seemed* like I was feeling things. I certainly had no trouble feeling sadness. I felt that intensely at times for many years after her death. But I never really let the anger come through. She had been suffering, after all. How could I be mad at her?

I was moody a lot and this irritated my mate. Years later, when I began to realize how much my mother's grief may have impacted her in my early years, I couldn't help but notice another pattern – how my life at that time was unfolding much like hers – my own unresolved grief interfering with primary relationships and blocking any chance of joy. Such is the pitfall of leading an unexamined life. We stumble on, following footsteps planted in our minds by the behavior of others, regardless of the negative outcome. Until, finally, we wake up to new insight, make the conscious choice to pursue life on a different path and undertake the journey, step by step.

Chapter Ten

Searching

A wise woman wishes to be no one's enemy;
a wise woman refuses to be anyone's victim.
~Maya Angelou

More than a year went by and I was still trying to make a life with Mr. Perlick. I woke up one day and realized I was spending my time washing the socks of a man who was never going to commit to me. I stopped using cocaine and, on the same day – in the same moment – made the decision to leave him and the house behind.

An acquaintance sensed my malaise and encouraged me to attend a personal development workshop that he had recently completed. I had the time and the money so I signed up and went. At the beginning, all participants were asked to agree to not use mind-altering substances for the duration of the weekend. I found out in advance that, by some quirky twist of fate, Mr. Perlick would be attending the same weekend as I was. I don't know if I was immediately aware that he was making his second pass at completing the workshop – having blown his sobriety agreement several weekends earlier. There we were, enrolled simultaneously in what ended up being a series of workshops designed to have us live lives from the simple perspective of what works and what doesn't. Later I learned the ONE Seminar was an offspring of the EST workshops that had been so controversial in the 1970s.

Without ever having the conscious intention to participate in the workshop at the same time, Mr. Perlick and I completed that weekend, followed up with the five-day intensive, then went on to the six-week program designed to support, educate and empower all participants to retool our lives for greater success and greater happiness.

That was the year I saved my life. Starting, as I said, from the question of what was working and not working in my life, I moved through a series of psychological growth experiences during which I dismantled my personality and assumed the active role of piecing it back together. I clearly remember experiencing a transformative visualization: lying on the floor of a large hotel conference room with about thirty other lost souls, I wandered back in my imagination through the years of my early adulthood, my teens, my childhood and all the way into my embryonic state. Quite literally, I was being given the chance to rebirth the true me. Tears flowed freely throughout the workshop, but I became even more acutely aware of their salty taste in those moments as I encountered the seed of my existence. With my two hands lovingly covering the middle of my chest, I focused on the beating of my heart. Workshop assistants were perplexed by my reluctance to remove my hands until I let them know how powerfully I was feeling the simple reassurance of the beat of my heart. The seminar leader, who was also something of a personal friend, came over and knew the profundity of my experience: "I am free!" After I quietly stated this truth, I was guided to an easel where I wrote those three words and signed my name, forming that unbreakable contract with myself: to live freely, unrestrained by fears and low expectations for my life

In that moment, *my life* began. I was no longer blindly following in my mother's footsteps and unconsciously recreating her misery for myself. I was free. Free from the relationship that had not (Thank

God) become a marriage; free from the expectation (that existed only in my mind) that I be a certain way because of the family name and ancestral heritage; free to explore my unique path to create for myself a life that I not only *wanted* to live, but would be thrilled to live. It was crystal clear to me in that moment that I could be, do and have so much more than I was about to settle for. This realization extended way beyond the material world. I knew without actually knowing the words at the time that I was awakening to my spiritual self; I was set to begin an adventure that would bring me abundant joy and prosperity. This life adventure would be measured in smiles and hugs more than in dollars and baubles.

In that time, it no longer mattered that my mother had chosen to put a gun to her head. That said nothing about me. I was a unique individual, no longer tied to her by cord or role. Yet I would come to understand that the work of healing my relationship with my mother would continue long into my life and long after her death. That healing would be both my teacher and my salvation. What I didn't realize was that these adventures in self-discovery usually involve some risk, some darkness and the courage to pass through times of despair, confusion and uncertainty. "The only way out is through." This was a catch phrase that I heard often in that time of workshops and self-discovery and I reminded myself of that truth quite often in the days, months and years that followed it.

In the fourth day of the second workshop, I was paired with a small group of other women and asked to create a performance that would get the other participants to stand up for us – a standing ovation for our authenticity, an experiential challenge to claim our power. We were given a song – the theme song from the movie *Cabaret* – that referred to the character, a corpse, being "laid out like a queen." I could practically see the casket and I felt the song had been chosen just for me. We worked out a very nice dance routine, threw together costumes and performed with skill and in sync with one another. No one got it. No one stood up. We tried again. But, much as I had wrapped up feelings in a tight, pretty package, the dance also was tight and pretty.

There we were, encircled by our comrades, knowing we wouldn't go anywhere until they stood up for us. Confusion and unknowing set in and only when I took the lead - even without knowing where we were going - in a spontaneous dance of enthusiasm, heart and soul expression, with the others following, did one person and then another and then the entire room stand up. I danced that day the joy I had felt when I made my "I Am Free" contract with myself. I danced the freedom to be more of who I am. And the others danced their unique dances. I had never known myself as a leader before and, even then, I did not experience it as a personal triumph or some kind of big win. I was just working to get the group objective met. Afterward we each collapsed into the waiting arms of six or seven of our comrades and were cradled and loved in a way I never had felt before. It was a stand-out experience of knowing that I was truly and deeply loved, not only by the human beings holding me, but by the Spirit that flowed through them to me, nourishing my very soul.

Somewhere in the midst of all this I came in touch with that part of me that very much wanted a child. I had not wanted to go that direction before. I even remember at age fourteen, announcing to my mother that I would never have children because I did not want to bring them into this messed up world. My mother cried that day and said she had felt the same thing. The baby craving was stirring in me though; I knew I had to listen to it, follow it, allow it to show me where I was going. I took the feeling literally and set out to find a suitable daddy.

As it turned out, I never did give birth. I eventually embraced the energy of this craving as I worked to rediscover my own inner child, the one who had gotten so lost trying to maneuver through a childhood alone. The child who grew up so quickly and then felt as lost as a little one again. But I had some journeying to undertake before I would get to meet that precious little girl.

The rest of that summer was devoted to the final phase of the workshop. I got my siblings involved, hoping this would heal the wounds that I intuitively knew we all had, although we never talked about them. My sister was experiencing confusion, possibly with some paranoia, and was struggling greatly. She seemed improved after the workshop. She was stable for a while, then chaos took over again. Medicines helped when she would take them consistently. I wanted to help but she wouldn't let me.

I made the decision for myself in those months to discontinue the anti-depressant medicines I had been taking for a couple of years. I did not consult the prescribing doctor, as I should have. I just stopped. I had stopped cocaine and pot that way; why not Elavil too? Much more recently, the doctors I have worked with in my professional role of counselor always advise patients to taper off anti-depressant medicines to avoid the flu-like symptoms that often come as withdrawal symptoms. I do not recall any flu symptoms, but did experience some altered perceptions for a few days. My brain felt like a photograph looks when it is mistakenly printed out of register. The blue, red and green are out of alignment and the image is like three images superimposed on one another but each off-center in a different direction. My brain certainly felt a bit askew! After a few days, my head cleared and I was then also free of reliance on medicines for symptom management. I convinced myself that I had dealt with the source of my distress during the seminar experience. I was well and whole. I thought.

Meanwhile the multi-generational wealth of my mother's family was drying up as fast as the West Texas grassland. The estate taxes forced financial decisions on my father that resulted in a significant reduction of assets. The economic downturn in Texas in the mid-1980s exacerbated the decline in value of what assets were left. The Harris family wealth, built over four generations, was evaporating before our very eyes and there was little to do about it. It was devastating and brought about many changes in very short order. Whether I liked it or not, whether I was ready for it or not, the situation was forcing me to reevaluate my skills, talents and abilities in order to find a career path that would sustain me. I had worked at several jobs but never pursued a career. I was working for my parents when my mother died and, looking back, it is obvious that I had outgrown that. So in the strange way that we would never actively choose for ourselves, the situation evolved and forced me - set me free - to truly find my passion and to pursue it.

As I was growing up, I was told from a very young age that I would never "have to work." That was part of our family culture; it was what my mother had known for herself and, therefore, it was what she wanted for us, her children. Before the ranch was taken from her, my mother may have thought her children would carry on the tradition of doing a little ranching, but mostly living off of assets. It seems like a fairytale, bubble world when I recall it now. It is all the more ironic when I think of how much my mother wanted to work instead of getting married at nineteen. But mine was the first generation of women truly empowered to work at more than subsistence and service-oriented jobs. I had the open invitation to move into new territories in the workplace. My mother did not.

It took several more years for me to fully comprehend my father's investment activities in the face of the dwindling assets. In addition to risky real estate ventures with the hope of large gains, he took large chances in the commodities markets. I am convinced the only one who wins in those markets is the broker who gets paid for every transaction. My father inherited the decision-making authority over estate assets when my mother died. He exercised it, managing assets for which he had not labored. The assets dwindled and then were gone. I think this was bound to happen because the principles of abundance and prosperity were not intact in my father's strategies. True wealth always involves an exchange - personal creativity is expended and another form of energy is gained - money, good health, dear friendships, philanthropic works, artwork, healing.

My father couldn't hold on to those assets because they weren't his. He had not utilized his considerable intellect to accumulate the funds he was investing. He was trained as a geophysicist, not an investor. He gave up that career, basically, to accompany and care for my mother by moving her back to her family home town where, I presume, the executive level positions for which he was qualified simply did not exist. The two of them made the decision that he would not work outside the home, that he would be a self-employed investor instead. By the time my mother died, he was no longer in the flow of prosperity because he was no longer giving of himself. Once he stopped caring for my mother, there was nothing for him to contribute in exchange for the funds he controlled. In that way, the flow of prosperity around him stagnated and went dead.

One internet search on the word "coach" will bring a thousand hits and tons of information about the nature of wealth and the laws of abundance and prosperity. I've come to understand that, of the many ways to measure abundance, money is the one form that gets most of our attention. Health is another form of prosperity; usually it is only recognized as such when it is not in good shape. Joy also flows to and through us and grows each time we recognize it for the free flowing energy that sustains and nurtures us as long as we care for ourselves well, live lives of meaning and rise above the burden of victimization. Creativity abounds within us when we live in balance and tend to our spiritual nourishment. Whether our finances are flowing in and out with ease or with constriction, we all live in the flow of prosperity. Simply by being born, each of us has a fund of talents and abilities, time and some degree of ability to connect with others. The generous giving of our talents, abilities, time and caring is perhaps the more accurate measure of our prosperity. As I searched for my right livelihood, I strived to discover how I could be of service in the world. That search led me away from job after job and eventually to a career that I love. I knew I was moving way beyond "having to work" into the uplifting realm of *getting to work* in ways that energize and thrill me - the true path to fulfillment.

The hardest lesson for me to learn was to stay in the attitude of prosperity even as my financial foundation liquefied beneath me. If we want prosperity, we must be prosperous in our attitude regardless of bank balance and other outward appearances. Continuing to give, even when we have little, is the way to enter into the attitude of prosperity. When we don't have cash to give, we can look to our other resources. Kindness, a beautiful singing voice, time spent reading to children, being a good Samaritan - we all have vast resources within us if only we have the mindset to tap them. Some would say they don't have time to volunteer. They may spend hours going to and from jobs that are routine and uninspiring. The first step is to find a way to give that fits in your life and lifestyle. From tiny trickles, mighty rivers flow.

I once paid a legal bill of over $500. by paying five dollars per month. Within about a year, I was able to pay more and quickly retired that debt. If I hadn't started to pay it off, it could very well still be with me today. I also learned to watch my prosperity language carefully, being certain to avoid affirming what I did not want. Affirmative or positive thought is a powerful tool. The difference between saying to myself, "I don't have the money for that" and "I choose to spend money on other things" is like night and day for the subconscious mind. Reminding ourselves of lack will bring more of it. At some point, the habit of affirming to myself the many forms of prosperity present in my life, including my finances, even when I wasn't feeling entirely secure about them, became part of me.

The workshops brought me these new understandings about prosperity and what really matters. I did spend some time and effort trying to get my father to see things in a new way. After the workshops, I came to understand that this was not my concern.

I stayed off the drugs, well the cocaine at least. I smoked some pot occasionally and was probably legally drunk several times per month. Like an addict, I minimized the impact of pot and alcohol, since I had stopped the *really* addictive substance. Bottom line, though, I had not yet faced the demons that underlie reliance on substance to cope with emotional pain. I felt the workshops had solved all of my problems, so I put my attention on finding work with meaning. A friend introduced me to a Unity church and I loved the little house in South Austin where Reverends Barbara and Tim Cook opened my mind even more to laws of spiritual reality. After about a year or two, I began to see a dream for myself – a new life in California as a teacher in some capacity. I was completely unaware that I was about to embark on the third geographical solution to my problems.

The workshops had piqued my interest in helping people discover themselves. Teaching appealed to me too, because of my new interest in children. I was looking to became a Waldorf teacher and found the training college was in Fair Oaks, California. In many ways, my decision to leave Texas was like throwing a dart at the map. I made plans to move to Fair Oaks, though I didn't know how I could afford to attend the Steiner College. I knew a little about Waldorf schools but had done virtually no reading in the discipline of Anthroposophy that forms their foundation. I now know I was acting from impulse, not plan. But I didn't know that at the time; I just knew I needed to leave home. I needed a dream to get me to move 1500 miles away without a job or any friends to greet me on arrival. What propelled me forward was the simple need to go into life, deeply and courageously, to find my own way. France might have provided that for me but France had been my father's dream for me, not my dream for myself.

CHAPTER ELEVEN

Take It To The Limit

*You are always protected as you step toward your
destiny. The universe will support you in your
purpose because it made you to fulfill it.*
~Yogi Bhajan

Now seven years out of college and six years since Mother died,
I left my roommate in charge of my condo in Austin, packed
up my hatchback and drove to California. I had been working for a
travel agent before I left Austin and had traveled on vouchers to Fair
Oaks to check out the area. I made arrangements to stay at a suburban
bed and breakfast which would be my base while I found longer term
housing. So I was prepared in some ways. Yet I was traveling (both
physically and spiritually) mostly on faith. A song that had played
a big part in One Seminar was *Take It To The Limit* by the Eagles.
Before I left Texas, at times when I was thinking intently about my
move, I would often find the radio playing that song. I took that as
guidance, an unseen source telling me to move forward with my
dreams - "put me on a highway and show me a sign." Ignorantly,
I took that to mean that all would be well in my new home. Easy
Street. But guidance doesn't always move us toward easy times;

genuine guidance only promises to move us toward greater awareness of who we are and toward a deeper awareness of the role of Spirit in our lives. I don't doubt that I was meant to relocate. I just wish I hadn't thought it was going to be simple.

That I was meant to go is illustrated for me most wonderfully by the way my car performed on the trip. I had a Honda Accord with about 50,000 miles on it. My brother had suggested that I change the oil before I left, but I didn't make time for that. Foolish. I had always relied on periodic service from the dealer but that had lapsed with my declining bank balance. I really did not fully understand the importance of frequently changing fluids in a car engine. Somewhere in Arizona, I stopped for gas and the attendant checked under the hood. The look on his face was quizzical and concerned as he approached me with dipstick and rag in hand to say, "Ma'am, there is no oil in your engine." I am sure I smiled when I said, "Oh! Could you put some in please?" That was certainly my "blondest" moment! I went on my way and the car performed flawlessly. Logic simply cannot explain why my engine had not burned up and left me stranded in the desert. But logic alone also cannot explain this arrival of true prosperity in my life when all that had changed was attitude and conviction. A consciousness of lack probably would have resulted in a melted engine on a hot day in the desert. I was new at developing my consciousness, but the miracle of my Honda punctuated how powerfully I was embracing the truth that attitude is the key to life.

I arrived in Fair Oaks, a community within the greater Sacramento metropolitan area. I found an apartment to share that was in the foothills of the Sierra Nevada mountains, about 30 miles out of town. The price was definitely right; it allowed me to live on about $500. per month for my first six months in California. This, once again, defied logic. If I had penciled out a budget, I don't think I would have been able to buy enough groceries. I went to Chamber of Commerce mixers with food. I met people and got taken to lunch sometimes. By the end of those six months I had found a job as a training manager for a professional association. My dreams of teaching at Waldorf schools had faded as I came to understand how much I would have to spend to get trained for a job that would offer starting pay of around $7.50 an hour. I decided adult education was a better path for me.

It was my first job in California and also my first experience working with a professional association. It was very difficult being the "foreigner" in that office. I found my coworkers to be unwelcoming to say the least. I was lonely for love anyway and became very lonely just for a friend I could rely on. The job went well for a while and then I began to chafe against a demanding boss and office politics that were unclear to me. I chose to leave even though I was asked to stay. Then I got another job with a company that went bankrupt a month after I started. I felt the bottom coming out of my life. I went to work for a bankrupt developer and had to find humor in how that was a mirror to my life. It was as if I were working once again for my father as he began his process of losing everything. Where had my prosperity consciousness gone? I wondered. I've since come to understand that consciousness is an ongoing discipline of thought, not a destination at which we arrive and then inhabit. I had some more lessons to experience, learn and move through.

CHAPTER TWELVE

Grief

*What a relief when you can realize that we're dying all the time
and being rebirthed again and again into our own lives, into the
heavens and hells that constitute our exquisite human experience.*
~Judith Orloff

When another bout of depression began to descend around me,
I realized that I had not yet dealt with the pain of grieving
my mother's death. I came across a book called *Silent Grief* and found
a monthly support group for survivors of suicide - the loved ones left
behind when a person succeeds in taking their own life. The Friends
for Survival monthly meetings were very intense for me. They took
place in a public meeting hall with participants seated in a circle. The
meetings opened with the invitation to introduce oneself and say
something about the death of the loved one. This meant, of course,
saying by what means they had committed suicide. There was so
much pain in that room. I had to pass when I first tried to say who
I was because the grief welled up and felt like it was choking me. I
don't know how I stayed for the whole meeting. But I did and I left
feeling very alone.

I remember more clearly being at an in-home meeting – a smaller, more intimate venue – where, by one of those non-accidents of life, the hostess was named Helen, just like my mother. She hugged me and I just broke out in tears. I could never explain to her why her hug had unleashed that dam of tears. For a long time, though, anyone's acknowledgement of my pain was enough to choke me up. The pain was ready to burst out, but I was still not able to share it in the relatively public environment of a home-based support group. It was progress, though, just to be feeling the pain.

Feeling despair and uncertain what to do next to "deal with it," I signed up for a weekend psychotherapy marathon that I thought would fix everything. I joined a group with nine other participants and we explored our problems together. We were, at various times, invited to "express ourselves" with a bat and a punching bag laid out on the floor. This was my first experience of the deep well of anger roiling in me about my mother's suicide. During that weekend, I came to terms with her decision by facing all of the feelings I had been running from – the rejection, the shame and guilt, the full sense of abandonment and the terrible heart-splitting rage at her for destroying herself. Suicide, the Final Fuck You.

At the end of the longest and most exhausting three days of my life, I thought I would be healed, good to go. Then, on Sunday evening, I had to look at the reality that my experience of growing up left me with behavioral patterns that would take some time to change. "Codependent" was a word I heard for the first time that day. In my journey through childhood and adolescence, in my unconscious attempt to save my mother, I had developed habits of taking care of others – doing for them things that they could and should do for themselves. That was how much I needed to control my situations. These behaviors were now ingrained in me and were, at times, compulsive, unconscious and annoying to others.

I also could no longer ignore that I had an alcohol problem of my own. That weekend I learned I still had an abandoned inner child within me who would only be completely healed as I surrendered to the process of letting go of both my addictions – alcohol and rescuing.

The end of those three days was also a necessary beginning. This was not a beginning filled with enthusiasm and promise, however. As much as I had felt renewed and invigorated by my spiritual awakening at the conclusion of the seminars three years before, I now felt discouraged, tired and not up to the task of undertaking another course of personal change. I was looking at night after night of Al-Anon meetings and maybe AA if I couldn't let go of my wine habit on my own. The undefined task of rescuing my inner child seemed impossible to me. Only my steady and consistent focus would get me through.

In Al-Anon, I courageously and meticulously unraveled aspects of my personality that were continuing to get in my way. I adopted the habit of rigorous honesty with myself. I challenged myself to identify my motives. I eventually trained myself to interact with others, not from an interest in rescuing them in order to feel good about myself, but from a place of true giving and compassion. I came to see the refreshing difference between a conversation in which I had some agenda to fulfill versus a simple exchange of ideas with no strings attached. I had to bust myself over and over again and was chagrinned at how much I had relied on manipulation to get what I wanted. I eventually came to realize how my sense of powerlessness and the indirect communication in my family had set the stage for me to learn to manipulate. I also had to own up to my tendency to displace anger - much of it left over from mother's death - on others. I had apologies to compose, amends to make, some crow to eat. I gradually began to accept myself as a less-than-perfect human being. I put away my whip (most of the time), forgiving myself for simply employing ways of coping which had worked for me in the past when I had no guidance on what else to use in the present.

At some point during this time, I made my first treasure map. My girlfriends and I got together to cut out images and words from magazines to put together a collage representing our dreams, the lives we each wanted to manifest for ourselves. Over the years, I made many of them, honing and refining the process of writing clear and specific vision statements and then illustrating them with a collage

I posted on my wall. More recently, these have come to be called vision boards. I imagine there are even apps to help create them in virtual form. The books that helped me in this - the most fun - part of the journey included *The Energy of Money* and *Building Your Field of Dreams*. I also found the little book, *Heal Your Body* around this time. I still have my first copy. It is tattered and even a little battered, from the times I threw it down, not yet ready to own what I had to own to get fully well.

I was unemployed for a while and then got hired as an administrative assistant with a very stable corporation. The salary was welcomed but my ego took a blow - secretarial work was so unsatisfying. I felt it was beneath me. Despite the progress in my healing in Al-Anon, I sank deeper into depression. I don't recall the time of year, but imagine it was probably fall or winter when I went home one day thinking I could take the Exacto knife from the office and use it to slit my wrists. Even through the fog of my depression, I knew it was time for me to get more professional help. I made the call to the crisis hotline to find a counselor.

At my first appointment, when I mentioned the Exacto knife, the therapist kind of tensed up her face with a concerned but perplexed expression and just looked at me for the longest time. I think her jaw even dropped a little. I don't think she knew what to do with a suicidal patient. I felt supremely self-conscious in that moment and quickly made arrangements to see a different counselor.

I found a wonderfully warm and motherly woman whom I liked from the start. I even found some enthusiasm for doing the work I needed to do with the assurance of individualized attention to my concerns. I continued to pursue my healing through Al-Anon and other avenues.

And I attended yet another weekend workshop. This one included a firewalk to be led by Peggy Dylan, a well-known facilitator of this ancient spiritual practice. When I signed up, I made sure the firewalk was optional - there was just no way I was going to walk barefoot on coals! In preparation for what was sure to be a life-changing event, Peggy simply led our group in a discussion, allowing us to ventilate all of our fears. A feeling of complete acceptance of all those considerations descended on the room. The light in the room - or my perception of it - even changed, becoming softer and more glowing.

We got in cars and drove to the fire. It was in the backyard of one of the workshop assistants. The night was crisp and cool; autumn. The bed of coals was about five feet wide by six or seven feet long. It had started as a large stack of timbers, about ten or twelve feet tall. Cedar, I believe. I was standing in a circle holding the hands of those next to me when I felt a jolt go around the circle and the man next to me released my hand. He was the first to walk across the coals.

Peggy had told us that if we were meant to walk that night, there would be a calm feeling in our stomachs. She had already described how the altered state of consciousness would allow us a window of time during which the embers would not burn us. She also said that as soon as we crossed the coals, she would be there to rinse our feet with the hose, since any embers that might stick on our feet could start to burn us after the walk, when we returned to our normal state of consciousness. I approached the fire and stayed for a long moment reading my feelings. I was tense all across my chest and I absolutely did feel fearful. But I recalled her words and knew that my gut and the rest of me felt very peaceful. I took a step and then another. Then I was across. It felt like walking on popcorn - the fire had degraded the small chunks of wood so that that they were pliable, almost soft. I felt no heat.

As I stepped off the coals I went into a momentary panic when I realized she was not spraying my feet with the hose! Then I looked down and realized I was standing in about three inches of water. I laughed at myself and she smiled oh-so-lovingly. I walked three times that night; others danced with partners through the coals. On my third time I noticed a tiny sharp feeling on my right foot and decided not to go again. As I recall my firewalk experience, I feel cradled in a pool of peace so complete that it defies description.

Firewalking is an ancient practice. Peggy Dylan is one of the people credited with bringing it back to this hemisphere from India. I imagine Native American practices included firewalking, but have never actually heard of that. One counselor explained the effect as opening up new pathways in the brain, allowing an expanded understanding of reality. The new pathways, he said, remain in the brain and allow firewalkers to create aspects of their lives that they might not have imagined before. It was all so inspirational. What I know for sure is that I did something I never imagined I would be able to do and no other single thing has had anything near the impact on my belief in myself, my confidence or my faith.

Yet, doors to my new life still did not open right away. I still had my personal work to do. I just approached it with a lighter heart and more conviction that I would get through it. I did decide I needed a new name for myself to go with the new person I was becoming. My given name, my family name – Helen Harris Willcockson – just did not fit anymore. Growing up, I was called Harris, as my mother went by Helen. Years later, my aunt figured out that the alcoholism in the family seemed to run through the Harris family line. I thought it would be a wise move to sidestep that legacy by calling myself by a different name. This was in the late 1980s and I was in the process of dating via voicemail – the precursor to internet dating. I took advantage of the anonymity and tried out some new names. Yes, I was a poser before I even knew that was a word! I finally landed on Tess after watching the movie *Working Girl*, where Melanie Griffith plays an administrative assistant who is misunderstood, with her intelligence unacknowledged. That struck a chord in me and I took the name for myself.

I worked in so many ways to resolve the pain of grief over my mother. I went back to the counselor who led the marathon weekend for an individual therapy session. With the bat and the punching bag in her office, I was able to dig down into the deep anger and fear that my mother would be reincarnated as a cockroach as punishment for the wasted life and violence she did to herself. I tried to imagine her lying down on the floor of her bathroom with the gun to her right temple. What could she have thought in those final moments? I raged at her actions. I raged at her addiction to alcohol. I raged at her abandonment of me. I raged at psychiatry that continued to treat her as she continued to drink, knowing even at the time that there was no other humane option for this woman who could not shake the habit. Eventually I raged even at God.

Somewhere along the way, I learned how to begin to forgive my mother for ignoring me in order to drink her misery away and then for leaving me entirely in order to finally end her pain. I found that EKG tape in my journal one night and sat with it for a moment, pondering. I built a fire in my fireplace, said some prayers, cried. Maybe I even laughed a little. Then I placed the paper on the fire. It melted more than it burned – the paper was heavily treated to allow the needle to slide over it and measure each heartbeat. The languid pace of its destruction seemed an appropriate ritual to acknowledge the seven long years it had taken me to begin to truly face and resolve the multiple layers and facets of grief I had felt for my mother.

Alcohol had left my lifestyle gradually throughout this period. For many years, though, I would still sometimes have a half a glass of wine, or toast with Champagne at someone's wedding. I always regretted it. Even when I didn't drink enough to even get tipsy or to cause a hangover, I began to notice that two or three days later I would be really irritable. When I first noticed this, I would go for acupuncture to make it better. It didn't take long before I really had to look at whether a half a glass of wine was really worth a $45. office-visit for needles in my liver meridian. I give great thanks for the insight that helped me put together the alcohol and the effect two days later. This marked the beginning of my ability to listen to and follow my intuition which would guide me more strongly and reliably to my healing … most of the time.

CHAPTER THIRTEEN

Realization

Y algo golpeaba en mi alma
(and something ignited my soul)
~Pablo Neruda

I was reading in my living room one day. Now in my mid-thirties, I had discovered a book called *The Courage to Heal*. It is a well-known book about sexual abuse and how to heal from it. My interest in the topic came out of my time in group therapy and the resultant realization that some of the psychological symptoms I experienced were similar to those of women recovering from childhood sexual abuse. That outrageous violation of the personal boundaries of women often brings about low self-esteem, lifelong troubles in relationships with men and other difficulties. As I read, I became aware of an odor that I immediately associated with my dog's poop. I was wondering why she had messed in the living room when I realized it could not have been the dog because I had given her away to a new owner about two months prior. There was clearly no fresh mess - no mess at all - in the living room that afternoon. As I pondered my confusion and continued to explore the odor, I discerned that it was not just the smell of feces, it was feces mixed with something else – something familiar, but strange – an earthy smell. Semen. I was fully experiencing the nauseating smell of the crotch of an unclean man. It amazed me that my senses could detect this odor that was not actually present with me in the room. The sensory experience was too strong to ignore. I wondered why, at that particular moment, this odor had manifested. That led me to wonder, if I had been molested, who had it been? What came into my mind next was the time in Iran when the car door came open and I went tumbling out.

While my family had chuckled at that story, I recall responding to it with a sort of numbing or disengagement. The question of what caused the incident haunted me until I explored it in a series of hypnotherapy sessions, eventually focusing on the question of what happened in the car that day. What surprised me about those sessions of hypnotherapy was that, instead of the point of view I expected (that of a detached observer), I saw the scene unfold in my mind's eye as though I were there. In that comfortable state of relaxation, the therapist regressed me back in time to my 3 year-old self. I saw the top of the car door where it met the bottom of the window. I saw the dashboard, wide and dark-colored. From that 3 year-old perspective, I saw my short toddler legs reaching just to the edge of the car's bench seat with my little-girl-feet in their shoes out there at the end. The car's dashboard, the inside of the passenger door and daylight coming in from the windshield above my head were the only other aspects of the scene I could see. I think I expected to see the scene as though it were a movie. But, instead, I was seeing it from the perspective of my tiny child self. Because of the perspective and how much it surprised me, I had no doubt that I had retrieved actual memory and not just metaphorical images (like dream images) which do often occur in hypnosis. The scene rang true to me.

I did not see the driver or any activity or details of mistreatment. At that time, in the early 1990s, there was much in the media about False Memory Syndrome – a very real and potentially dangerous phenomenon where the therapist can inadvertently implant impressions in the mind of the client with leading questions. I did not want to jump to conclusions and get all dramatic about what I experienced in hypnosis on the topic of molestation. But it lingered with me, that suspicion. Part of me did not want to know any more than I had seen that day in hypnotic trance. But part of me also already did know that something must have happened in that car with that driver. Over time, I just came to assume that I had been molested and began to work through the issues that this implied: where were my parents and why was I not protected? These questions, in fact, drove much of the searching, the answers and the healing that are recounted in this book. A great deal of this healing took place before I became certain that the family employee had, indeed, taken advantage of me.

My suspicions were validated almost ten years later during the last lucid conversation I had with my sister. She mentioned how the Iranian chauffeur had "bothered" her and she wondered if he had tried to bother me, too. We spoke of these things briefly and not in direct terms. The fact that he had molested my older sister, along with my spontaneous olfactory memory, were sufficient confirmations for me. I never pursued discovering exactly what he may have done or tried to do to me. I've never needed to know those details. I just needed to know how to heal.

Over the next several years, I would come to understand more about molestation, victims and perpetrators; how often molesters are somehow close to the family and/or attempt to endear themselves to the family to gain access to victims; how much they will work to hold on to such relationships, once established. With that information, the oddly shaped pieces of my story began to form a comprehensible whole picture of a child harmed, or at least threatened with harm, by a foreign man who, for many years, maintained contact with the rich Americans.

My healing took place in spite of him. Initial forgiveness came to me in the notion that he was a man who had not been trained by his society to direct his sexual energy in a loving way. Much later still, the opening sequence of the film *Argo* gave me a broader and deeper perspective on his crime. The film suggests that the Shah's assumption of power in Iran was at least endorsed by the

U.S. Presumably, American greed for oil coincided with Iranian governmental deprivation and near starvation of the vast majority of Iranians while the Shah and the elite in Iran lived in opulence and, perhaps, abject waste - if it is true that the Shah, even once, had his lunch flown in from Paris.

With that awareness, I had to look once again at the motives of this man my parents had trusted to drive for us. I presume he was young, perhaps in his twenties, with the opportunities for him to create a life of his dreams severely curtailed by political circumstances beyond his control. One way to respond to this powerlessness in life could have been to take something - anything he could - from the Americans who were taking so much from him and his country. When the freedom to be, to speak and to move toward one's life dreams is stilted by oppressive political circumstances, then the ways of communicating become behavioral. What better way to act out against the Western supporters of Iranian misery than to molest their children?

Sexual gratification is one motive, but probably only rarely the whole picture. Sexual abuse is always a power play. This new understanding of that hired driver's possible motives forced me to look again at the impersonal hatred it seems to imply. With crystal clarity, I could finally see that the things he may have done or tried to do to me had nothing to do with the person I was, or with the person I am. This deeper understanding of the forces at work in his culture does not compel me to condone his molestation of me. It doesn't change the truth of my innocence. It does not make me or my family in any way responsible for his choice to target me. It doesn't make it right. It makes it forgivable.

He is probably dead by now. Who knows if he harmed others beyond our family, but most molesters would have. I can only hope his soul's lessons were completed in some way and that his next life is one of greater compassion and service to humankind.

Early in my therapy I had been encouraged to continue my education. Without knowing how I would pay for it, I submitted my application for graduate school at California State University at

Sacramento on the very last day possible for admission in the following semester. In the Fall of 1990 I started to train as a psychotherapist. I worked weekends and attended classes on weekdays. I went to work for about $7. an hour as a staff member in a children's group home – those modern day orphanages for kids with emotional disturbances. It was stressful, tiring and I was often afraid of the kids whom I sometimes helped to physically restrain. That was the best training possible for me as the aspiring family therapist. I had not met that prince who would be father to my own children. I needed to gain the experiential understanding of the rigors and exhaustion that come with parenting irrational little humans.

The end of my second semester of grad school corresponded with the tenth anniversary of my mother's death. I was wrapping up my therapy and I wanted to design a personal memorial for my mother that would punctuate my blossoming acceptance of her – her life and her final choice. The process of therapy had shown me so clearly that what my mother taught me was mostly indirect – just as our family communication was mostly indirect. I felt she had primarily taught me how *not* to live. But as the woundedness receded and my heart opened into healing, I came to know the value and quantity of things she *had* taught me that I had taken for granted. On May 30th, 1991, I went to the American River with a large and expensive (especially on my student budget) bouquet of yellow roses I had bought several days before. I had enjoyed them and felt the expanding buds signaled a new way for me to carry in my heart the imperfect yet loving mother she had been to me.

I found a happy memory to associate with each blossom as I dropped it from the bridge and watched it float to the bend of the river where I could see it no more. I remembered how much she loved to swim; I could feel my little hands holding on to her strong shoulders in the sunny pool when we were both so young. I could see her singing in the car on the way home from the ranch, a large thunderhead out the window behind her, light streaming out from behind it, just as it had that day on our front porch when she taught me the awesome beauty of a Texas storm in the late summer.

I struggled with the last few flowers to find hopeful memories powerful enough to replace those spots within me that had held on so tightly to the sad, hurtful things. I believe this private memorial set in motion an eventual cascade of positive memories rediscovered. I reviewed many of our times together and opened once again to that love she had given me. As I reset my heart and mind to hold onto the goodness of my mother, I was also resetting my life to capture the goodness that Spirit holds for me.

In the final year of my graduate training, I worked as an intern art therapist in a local psychiatric hospital. I offered art therapy to individuals and groups of children and adults with psychiatric diagnoses that ranged across the spectrum. After only a couple of months of this work, I began to have trouble sleeping. It didn't take long for this to severely impact my ability to function, so I went to an acupuncturist for help. He treated me and also perceived something more was impacting me, causing the disrupted sleep. Knowing that I was spending time in close physical proximity to persons with severe mental illness, he suspected I would benefit from instruction in how to protect myself from those energies. He referred me to Michael Tamura who offered a six-week class on Psychic Healing of Self and Others. Though I barely could scrape together the fees for the class, I knew I had to do it. So, before I got into trouble for missing my intern duties due to sleep deprivation, I signed up and quickly gained tools for self-clearing that were essential to my success for many years.

I learned to use an image of a flower – I chose the rose – to retrieve my own energy that had become dissipated throughout the day. I took it back from individual people, places and situations, like the person who seemed to demand so much of my attention or freeways I had been driving on, or some focus of worry I had spent too much time on that day. I took back my own energy from anywhere I could imagine and put it in the rose. Then, I would explode the rose in my imagination and actually feel the energy re-entering my being at the top of my spine and the brain stem.

Another technique focused on dispelling the energy of others which had invaded my space and was drawing me down or, in the case of sleep troubles, ramping me up for no reason of my own. In those cases, I would see the rose absorbing those energies and, as I blew the rose up in my mind's eye, those energies were released back to the cosmos, clearing my field in the process.

Finally, I learned to use the rose to scan my interior and remove unwanted energies from unknown sources and then move the rose out of my body, blow it up and experience the lightness that came from unburdening myself. At times, I am convinced I was able to ward off minor illness this way and it certainly helped keep me clear, able to focus and, thankfully, able to sleep!

I relied on this meditative process for self-healing for many years. Along with Transcendental Meditation, these practices of exploring my inner planes of existence protected me and also gave me a great respect for the role that unseen energies play in overall health and outlook.

(Curiously, though, after close to 15 years of self-clearing, a psychic consultant told me she saw me with millions of tiny shards of energy floating in my aura. From that point on, I carefully directed blown-up energy down into the earth to be transmuted rather than continuing to hang out with me.)

Before I graduated, I took a required course on the use of psychological assessment instruments. One of my classmates gave a presentation about post-traumatic stress disorder (PTSD.) I don't even recall now which particular assessment instrument was our focus that evening. I do remember clearly sitting in that classroom suddenly overwhelmed and completely distracted by a flood of memories about that tall, blonde Frenchman - Monsieur Moustaches. Several years after my time in France, when I could no longer remember his actual given name, I had made up a name for him. I began to think of him as Jean-Luc. Sitting in the classroom that night though, his actual name was suddenly clear and sure: Denis. As I said his name in my mind, a smile came across my face. And even as I write about him, I feel the connection all over again. Another dead person whose presence in my life, however brief, seems perfectly purposeful now in that he caused me to learn to open to love again even after the pain of the loss. I might have learned this lesson through a breakup but how much more fully I learned it through his passing. I know that he knows how grateful I am for the catalyst that he was in my learning to live and daring to love.

As part of my effort to find the man of my dreams (I refer to this as my time of the ten thousand coffee dates), I met a man who seemed to fit the bill except that he was quite aloof. We had coffee several times and then dinner. He was stable and even wealthy. I thought he would make a fine father for my children and I had it all planned out. We had similar spiritual interests and ended up organizing a workshop to be offered at his house. I invited some folks I was working with and enjoyed the day enormously. A couple of weeks later, I learned that he was dating one of the women I had invited. Neither of them had said anything to me, even though I was in close touch with both of them. My heart was once again broken.

This was the first time I had experienced the awful betrayal by a girlfriend. I cried my eyes out and then got on my knees one night to let God know that I was finished looking for Mr. Right. I had one more semester of graduate school, I told God, and I was going to just focus on my career as a therapist. I had told myself many times that I was done with looking and seeking and striving for that one relationship that would end my loneliness. That night, though, I knew it was real and true. I totally let go. I felt in my depth that I was going to be just fine on my own. I was alone but no longer lonely. I had found a purpose for my life. I was completing the training I needed to live that purpose. That was my life companion.

CHAPTER FOURTEEN

Surrender

Surrender doesn't mean giving up. It means giving in
to the path and destiny you were born to take.
~Yogi Bhajan

Six weeks later, I went to a church service alone on New Year's Eve. I amused myself by watching people as they came in. A dark-haired man entered the room on the far side, walked all the way to the front and then back down the nearby aisle to settle in a seat directly in front of me. Of course I didn't have any interest in pursuing this very nice-looking man; I had told God I was done looking! Yet the man caught my attention.

The lesson at the service, given by Reverend Cherie Larkin, was about relationship - about how, once entered, a relationship never really ends and never completely stops affecting us because we still have interaction with our memories of that relationship. Toward the end of the lesson, the minister - following a tradition in that Unity church - passed the microphone around and asked for positive affirmations for the New Year. I had never had any desire to grab the microphone before. That night, however, I decided to boldly affirm "excellent health and abundant energy as I complete my last semester of graduate school!" I had the mic in my hand and started to speak when tears came and choked me up.

Don't we all just love to lose it and cry in public? How embarrassing! Determined, but unable to speak because of the lump in my throat, I simply whispered my affirmation into the mic. Then I got rid of it as fast as I could! I was feeling very small and hot with embarrassment. The man seated in front of me turned around and handed me a tissue as I sat back down. I smiled gratefully and noticed what gentle eyes he had. I seriously considered just running out of there and heading home to a solitary midnight. But, instead, I went to the ladies' room, pulled myself together and stayed for the party, which promised Dances of Universal Peace - a kind of spiritual square dancing - followed by game night.

The Dances involved slow, prayerful movements in two concentric circles such that a person in one circle will dance with everyone from the other circle eventually. And there he was in the other circle! Each time we danced, I marveled at his open willingness to allow me to look deeply into his eyes - those gentle eyes - and down into the immensity of his soul. He told me his name. Michael.

We sat together for a game or two. I made sure he had my phone number that night before I left the party early, wanting to be home before the drunks hit the road. He called to invite me to coffee, after waiting the requisite two or three days. As we sipped our coffee, it seemed we each had a clipboard, checking off the other candidate's qualifications for the role of lover/mate. Then came an afternoon at the park. Then dinner at his house. We explored our dreams and found ourselves moving in similar directions in life. We didn't rush to intimacy but he kissed me eventually and I knew I would marry him. He proposed in November and we were married the following July. Bliss. And every bit worth the long, long wait.

His family members welcomed me and have come to love me as their own. Without ever experiencing the mystery, challenge and joys of motherhood, I learned I would soon become a grandmother. Several months later, we were driving together to go visit his daughter who had recently given birth to our first grandchild. As I was riding along with my husband, looking out the window at the sound wall of the freeway, I realized, for what seemed like the first time since my childhood, I was smiling for no particular reason.

CHAPTER FIFTEEN

Acceptance

Work is love made visible.
~Kahlil Gibran

Throughout these years of coming into my own, I had finally given thoughtful consideration to what profession I was to pursue, what I would do with my life. We are, so often in this American culture, defined by what we do for a living. In my struggle to become who I am, I thought that what I would *do* for a living would cause me to *have* material things and even spiritual understandings that would empower me to *be* the person I believed I could become.

I had it backwards. Appropriate self-esteem, and probably good mental health in general, rests on the acceptance that we are each valuable just for being. We are, after all, human beings not human doings. The better way to progress into adulthood is to be supported from the earliest age in discovering and pursuing the impulse to be the person we were born to be. With the guidance of thoughtful parents, children are encouraged to explore their own personality attributes, interests, strengths, and also to experience failures and live through them to arrive at a solid sense of that person they are meant to become. Out of this comes a natural progression to do the vocation and avocations of interest. "Have" comes at the end. A solid sense to *be* oneself, combined with a personal awareness of the capability to *do* things to contribute to society leads a person to *have* their needs met and to have a life that suits them.

There still are times in my life when I feel off track. The be-do-have principle is usually within whatever bits of wisdom that bring me back on course.

For my wedding, I chose an old Nat King Cole song, *Nature Boy*. My dear friend, Jennifer, sang it beautifully and the song said it all: "The greatest thing we'll ever learn is just to love and be loved in return."

I had spent all of my life seeking the love that seemed just beyond my grasp. It was only when I had arrived at the place of accepting myself as I am that my husband with his great love appeared in my life. When he proposed that day by the river, I felt as though I had finally received my reward for the hard work of remaking myself. The spot on the riverbank that he chose was a beautiful little point of land arching out into the American River. It was near our home and we visited that spot on the river several times before and after our wedding. In the last few days of 1996, a cold storm came through and dumped tons of snow in the Sierra. The holiday skiers and snow bunnies were delighted. Then just a few days later, a very warm storm from the tropics, locally known as a "Pineapple Express," came through with days of rain that melted snow into floodwaters that raged down the regional rivers. It was as if liquefied mountains were washing into the Sacramento Valley.

That precious little point of land where he proposed to me washed away in those floods. I remember my confusion when we walked down to find our spot. We waded across a low spot on the trail, through some standing water, then asked ourselves if we had taken a wrong turn or whether we were looking in the wrong spot. We soon realized how changed the area was; our spot had melted into the water, flowed out toward the San Joaquin River Delta and into the San Francisco Bay beyond. I remember the twinge of sadness followed by a concern that this might somehow be a bad omen. I dismissed the bad omen interpretation immediately, preferring the understanding that rivers, like time, do not stand still. Destruction in one spot is a necessary ingredient of creation in another.

Perhaps Michael's love for me is like the river too. As it has flowed into me, it has filled the gaping hollows as well as the little eddies of my soul. It has gradually eroded the painful memories of things beyond my control while it continually deposits deeper love and acceptance of myself - like nacre on a pearl. I had done the preliminary work of repairing my self-esteem before I met Michael. Knowing in my heart that I am a good person with gifts to share with the world is the larger gift, or end product, of my time of self-realization. Having the truth of my goodness reflected back to me by this man who is my hero, has deepened my capacity for love of myself and others. My husband's love, though, has shored up my confidence in ways I believe I was never going to achieve on my own.

This could never have happened in the reverse order. In fact, I spent much of my life trying to find someone else who could love me enough that I wouldn't have to do the hard work of coming to love myself. But once I had built the foundation of self-love, I attracted to myself that which I knew to be true in my core: that I am truly lovable. Then the love could only flow more abundantly to me.

When I began my eighteen months of therapy just before graduate school, I made a list of events that helped me understand the circumstances of my early years. It is significant that I began the list with events that took place before I was born. Much of the focus of the project was on my mother's state of mind during her pregnancy with me and beyond. Enmeshment is a clinical term used to describe a relationship where two people become melded together, psychologically speaking. Children of alcoholic parents are often enmeshed with the parent, meaning that the children take on adult-level responsibilities for the parent who cannot function as expected because of the illness of addiction. Child does for parent what parent should do for self and for child. Child does not develop a sense of being a separate entity, but rather begins to take on the experience of the adult even to the point of feeling the feelings of the adult. Child then eventually may fail to separate the adult's feelings from the child's own feelings.

One of the four tasks of grieving involves emotionally relocating the deceased. This entails letting go of the loved one and preparing to continue on without their physical presence. My process of healing was intricately wrapped up in my letting go of responsibility for my mother, which had its roots in our enmeshment. As I grappled with this task, I would see her, in my imagination, in the moments before she made the terrible choice to shoot herself. I always saw her lying passive and helpless on the floor of the bathroom with the gun at her right temple. After all, that is where the blood had been when I went in to clean; there were blood spatters, too, on the wall, down low by the floor. She had spent so much time in bed that imagining her lying there on the floor was totally in keeping with my experience of her. And for all those years and through all of that healing, that was the image I came back to.

Late in the process of writing this account, however, nearly 20 years after her death, I finally came to see that she didn't lie down on her bathroom floor. That was where she fell afterward. That means she stood in front of her mirror and saw the reflection of herself as she pulled the trigger of the .22 pistol. Many have called suicide the coward's way out. It certainly is the act of running from something. I don't wish to aggrandize it here. My mother's action, though, wasn't from cowardice. It came from being simply worn down by unrelenting pain, weary of the struggle to overcome it and, perhaps even her awareness that her intractable sadness was creating a burden for her family.

Now, when I think of her standing there in front of the mirror, I see her facing herself with, yes, some measure of desperation but also with courage and the fear that always underlie bravery. For my mother, Hell was not some place she would go when her life was through. Hell was the place where she had lived most of her adult life. I no longer have any fear that she is paying or will pay some kind of penance for her action. I do believe that growth of her soul depends on her mastering the challenges that she avoided this time around. They will be here waiting for her in her next incarnation. That, I believe, is her only "penance."

The soul grows regardless of our choices. It is our choices, however, that determine the direction of that growth. I no longer blame my mother or hold any resentment for her choice to end her life. Despite the years of numbness, searching and the painful loneliness of my grieving process, my own journey to forgiveness and resolution has shaped me and strengthened me. It has made me who I am and I am grateful for that becoming.

Do I wish that these realizations had come to me sooner? That certainly would have made for a different life. But my husband and I have often mused at how, if we had met even a year before we did, we probably would not have cared much for each other and may not have felt any attraction at all.

We can't push the river. We do well to simply let go and enjoy the flow.

Chapter Sixteen

Next Level

> *... you strode deeper and deeper into the world,*
> *determined to do the only thing you could do –*
> *determined to save the only life you could save.*
> ~Mary Oliver

On Memorial Day of the year when Mother had been gone from my life as long as she had been in it, I gathered my five best friends with me at the river and released a single white rose into the current. We all watched it float until it was gone as I explained that the one rose was for the gratitude I finally have learned for the life she gave me. I felt complete.

She died at age 53 and around five months. I was aware of the numbers long before I turned 53. I wondered how I would move through the milestone of becoming the age that my mother was when she died. Like it or not, she was my role model. I felt certain I would never die by my own hand. I had prayed for a long, healthy and happy life with my husband. I had dedicated myself to self-care regimens that supported that.

In anticipation of my fiftieth birthday, I decided to put some changes in place in my life. I had noticed a decline in my energy level over the previous several years. The complaint of fatigue, coupled with a history of several mild depressive episodes, led my mainstream doctor to a diagnosis of depression and proposed treatment with anti-depressant medicine. I didn't have any other symptoms of depression - sadness, lack of interest in things or a decline in my personal hygiene. I just had less energy than I thought would be normal. I was mindful of the Seasonal Affective Disorder (SAD) that had colored many of my autumns and winters. I may have had a mild seasonal depression, but I felt that diagnosis did not satisfactorily explain all of my concerns.

I also did not want to put my body through the ordeal of taking anti-depressant medicines. A few trials of different medicines at various times since my teens had never been successful - the troublesome side effects of intense headaches, parched mucous membranes throughout my body and the terribly uncomfortable akathisia always outweighed the benefits of the medicine.

I decided that a regular program of exercising would help. So I pushed myself out the door to walk three mornings per week. Soon I began to feel the positive results of the consistent aerobic exercise. Walking turned into running and I enjoyed it. I watched my diet carefully, since certain foods seemed to cause lung congestion that was diagnosed as asthma. The symptoms cleared up when I completely eliminated wheat, corn and dairy products from my diet. I read a book called *The Mood Cure* and worked with a practitioner to gently shift the chemical balance away from depression, which was present. I made the decision to start running in the early spring - the time of year when I would typically be coming out of the (SAD) funk that starts with the change in light and the shortening of the days in the preceding autumn.

In addition to daily self-clearing, I also meditated daily, as I had fairly consistently since learning Transcendental Meditation in the early 1980s. I was working in the department of psychiatry of a health maintenance organization in the Sacramento area. My job demanded a lot of energy and compassion. Working as a mental health counselor is never a walk in the park. Yet, as long as I tended to my self-care through meditation, good diet and exercise, I managed the stress effectively and enjoyed my work. Then the interpersonal dynamics among the staff disrupted that flow. The job offered security, though, and I was reluctant to leave it.

In 2005, my attention was diverted elsewhere. With the things I would be facing and coping with over the next two years, a job change would have been nearly impossible anyway. I coped with the mounting stress of the job I had, but I didn't necessarily cope well. I relied heavily on the benefits of positive thinking and affirmative prayer of my Unity church as I dug even deeper within myself to find that capacity – the capacity that is within everyone – to maintain a positive outlook even in the face of difficult circumstances.

Unity had been my church since before I left Texas. In Sacramento, though, it took on a whole new dimension when two amazing ministers took the plunge and founded a new church called Spiritual Life Center. Reverends Faith and Michael Moran brought unequalled vibrancy and inspiration to the ministry. It was so easy to love them and support their mission to Love, Serve and Remember ... to love, serve and ...

Faith had been given the privilege and responsibility for production and sales of jewelry and other items depicting the Oneness Symbol, a peace sign for the 21st Century which incorporates the symbols of the seven most prevalent religions in the world now. Oneness Ministries continues to spread the word and energy of humanity's oneness, harmony and craving for peace through the Oneness jewelry, publications, speaking engagements and spiritual travel tours.

A few years into the growth of Spiritual Life Center, as the entire congregation floated along, in love with these two amazingly gifted and giving spiritual leaders, dreaded news arrived. Faith, after struggling for months with unreliable cognitive functioning, learned she was in the early stages of a rare form of dementia. She demonstrated such poise and grace when she talked with us about the diagnosis as simply something that had washed up on her beach. The long slow loss of this lovely woman was made easier by her last message from the podium, which included this bit of wisdom: "Give me your faith, not your fear."[126] She did not need all 600 of us trying to take care of her; she wanted us all praying for and with her. I think we each did our best to honor that as this loving couple, to whom we had all looked for support and guidance through difficult times, faced a life hurdle I could barely wrap my mind around.

Our thriving and vibrant congregation seemed to hold its collective breath as she went through months and then several years of an agonizing decline. She died at home, in 2008, with loved ones near, most notably her heartbroken husband, Michael Moran.

It was August of 2005, when Hurricane Katrina roared across the Gulf of Mexico toward New Orleans. My father and his second wife (of many years) evacuated their tiny apartment in that lovely city, accidentally leaving one of his five emphysema medications behind. They went to Austin to stay with a welcoming relative but, it saddens me to say, the city did not treat them with kindness. My father's insurance did not cover him outside the state of Louisiana, except for emergency care. He had to rely for several months on rotating emergency room doctors who probably did their best. My father's health had been declining already, but the lack of consistent care probably sped up that process. He felt it best to return to his doctor in New Orleans.

In January of 2006, they went back to an apartment, sight unseen, that had been "renovated" after the flooding. Under the new paint were molds and mildew that contributed greatly to my father's last hospitalization. He was cared for with kindness and great compassion by not only his wife, but also his doctor and the hospital staff. I visited him in early March, arriving the day after the end of Mardi Gras. As we drove down trash-strewn St. Charles Avenue, I was shocked by this grand city's fall from grace: shuttered windows everywhere; grass struggling to come back in the medians that had exuded such grace and ease. Even the armrests on the little zebra-striped couch in our hotel room told the story with the grime ground into the fabric by hands working hard to repair so much that had been destroyed. My husband and I made pre-arrangements for my father's eventual cremation. That took us through the Ninth Ward, the area that was hardest hit by Katrina and Rita. Flood waters had overtopped and then destroyed the levee built by the U. S. Corps of Engineers. The floods in that area took out homes - some of them off their foundations - that had been occupied by people least able to cope with such ruin. Desperation was everywhere. My father was in an intensive care unit, eyes closed, unaware of our presence, with breathing and feeding tubes - exactly the scenario that I hope to never experience for myself.

My brother came with his two sons whom I had not seen since they were teens and had served as ushers at my wedding. We were all on Magazine Street having dinner one evening when I made a reference to "the boys." The younger nephew smiled when he said to his brother, "Listen, the old lady is telling us what to do!" I got it. Since they were now approaching thirty, it was probably a good time for me to find a new context for them. That night I dubbed them the "fine young men." The phrase stuck and now brings a chuckle at times.

After a few days, it was time for me to head to the airport, to go back home, to get back to work. Dad opened his eyes - only once. I was able to see those sparkling blue eyes one last time. I told him goodbye in a whisper, saying all I needed to say: "I love you. You are a fine man." I had always loved him, but I had to acknowledge that the man lying on the hospital bed was a very different person from the man who went up the stairs that Memorial Day in 1981 after hearing the gunshot, and then called me and asked me to stay with him in those first few unreal hours. He had enjoyed a complete second life in his marriage after my mother died. He coped with the reversal of his fortunes, having lost the entire estate my mother left. Financial security dwindled away during the recession of the 1980s and then was gone completely soon after. My father lived his final years in a tiny flat in New Orleans with his wife who loved him truly. His subsistence income came in the form of a modest Social Security check. Oddly, I think those years were some of his happiest.

Back in California and back at work, I spent nightly time in prayer with him across the fifteen hundred miles that separated us. He died about six weeks later, on Good Friday. I got the call late and went into the living room to rest and absorb the reality of the news. I was listening to music through headphones. Lying there on the couch with angelic voices in my ear, I felt his presence off to my right and a little behind me. I was so startled by the sensation of it - it was so clear. Startled, but pleased. I sat up and turned to face him. I smiled and cried at the same time, so relieved that he was no longer lying in a hospital room, suffering with bedsores and feeding tubes.

"It's okay." I said to him several times. What I meant was, it's okay to let go, to float free. I felt so blessed and privileged to have had this opportunity for one last chat with him. The sweetness of it is beyond words, but resides as a glow in the center of my chest. Later, I read that when departing souls make these visitations, it takes a lot of precious energy. The connection I had always felt with my father is reflected in my belief that he made the effort to drop in on me that night. It calls me to wonder what more was detailed in that contract we made before I was born, when I chose him to parent me. Clearly we have danced this dance before in different ways, in different lifetimes.

Once again, I had grief to work through. I thought my grief for him was fairly uncomplicated. I thought I would move through it fairly quickly, fairly easily. Any resentments I had of him were long ago forgiven and forgotten. This was the man who had been both father and mother to me since my mother's ability to parent was fading dramatically by the time I was really growing up.

Yet, now I no longer had living parents. That is always a somber realization. Even though it seemed, clinically speaking, uncomplicated, this grief exhausted me; it sapped whatever energy I had left. I felt so tired, I was no longer able to get myself out to run or even walk for exercise. I managed to get to work and continued to do a good job in less than ideal circumstances. Most evenings I dragged myself to the kitchen to make dinner then collapsed on the couch until I could go to bed. I woke often in the night and couldn't fall asleep again. My nightly hours of sleep started to dwindle, compounding the exhaustion.

Even as my father's decline had been unfolding, my father-in-law, Bill, was coping with dementia. Lewy-body dementia was suspected but could not be confirmed until after he passed. His record probably showed Alzheimer's disease. A major difference between the two is that Alzheimer's patients often have personality changes that can result in aggression, even towards loved ones whom they may or may not actually recognize at any given time. Bill never had outbursts. He was always very quiet and gentle, even when he became anxious or confused. My mother-in-law was an absolute rock for him, answering his repetitive questions with patience and kindness.

Bill had a medical procedure that resulted in an infection that was treated with antibiotics which, we later learned, caused disorientation. He went to the emergency room and then stayed in the hospital for several days. He was later released to a skilled nursing facility where he stayed for about six weeks. When he was finally able to return home, my husband talked his mom into having in-home care for four hours each day to help Bill get up, get showered and go for a short walk to regain some of the strength he had lost due to the infection and hospital stay.

I can't pinpoint the time when he stopped recognizing me, but I became aware of it gradually and had to slip to the background of the life of this man whom I had come to love as my own. I still visited often when my husband went - about three days per week. As I grieved my own father's passing, I witnessed my father-in-law's decline. He went into a care home in May and declined further immediately. That is probably a likely outcome with any transition away from the elder's familiar environment. It didn't help that the care home failed to give him his dementia medication for the first ten days. Got to watch those folks like a hawk!

Bill died in August of 2007. My husband was sitting there reading as his sleeping father took his last breath. A peaceful surrender; a huge loss. This was the first major loss for my husband and his family. We lived close to his parents and we had taken the lead in helping "Mom" manage hospital and other care decisions. Bill's three daughters put together the memorial service and did a magnificent job of setting up the room and laying out a banquet worthy of the celebration of a well-lived life. When it seemed that everyone had arrived, I asked one of the sisters who would be running the program if she had planned to say a few words. Startled by the prospect, her eyes flew open wide and she slowly shook her head. She thought Michael and I were in charge of that. I asked one of the grandchildren to take the podium. She was willing and able - for a few minutes. She got teary and it was clear that she just needed to be a participant. I looked around and saw there was a job that had to be done with no one else to do it. Whether I came from obligation, a desire to be helpful or a place of knowing I had the skill to lead the event is not really clear to me. I took the microphone, though, and invited stories about Bill. There were tears and laughter and the gathering went well. It provided everyone the opportunity to grieve and say a little bit of a goodbye to this kind and generous man. At the end, Bill's grandson told the story of Bill in a submarine during World War II, waiting in tense silence until he heard the whizzing sound of an enemy torpedo barely missing their hull. Bill had been *that* close to almost everyone in the room never being born.

As I had done for several months, I simply went from this event to whatever was next on my schedule. I had lost any real conscious connection to what was going on in my life. I was sleep deprived and felt so tired, generally, that I just put one foot in front of the other to keep going. Had I been more aware at the time, I would have realized that facilitating a memorial service is like being a lightning rod for the emotions as people choose to speak their stories and their sadness. Lightning rods ground electricity. As emcee, I was struck by the strong feelings, but had not allowed all of that energy to pass all the way through me. It took a while for me to realize I needed to take action to move that grief - the grief of others - out of my system. This tendency to take on the emotions of others began to plague me even more and I struggled to understand by what mechanism that could actually happen and by what means I could undo the effect it had on me.

Over these months, having abandoned my habit of daily meditation, I believe I also began to hold on, unconsciously, to residues of the distress and anguish my clients were expressing in my office. Since my father's death, my meditations had not taken me to the calm, restorative places of serenity I had known over the past twenty years. Instead, my meditations were twenty-minute episodes of worry thoughts and stormy inner seas. The most self-defeating choice I have ever made was to stop meditating because I couldn't get to the calm. The stormy times are when we need the meditation the most. I knew this but simply could not will myself back into the regular habit of meditation. I did not yet fully realize how much meditation was an essential ingredient in my ability to continue to succeed as a counselor.

I was feeling worse and worse. My sleep was disrupted every night. I would wake with more of the worry thoughts and distress that kept me from meditating. Unsatisfied with my mainstream doctor's perpetual return to the diagnosis of depression as the cause of my fatigue, with anti-depressant medicines as the only treatment plan, I returned to the naturopathic doctor whom I had seen intermittently over the previous ten years. We looked again at diet and I made some more adjustments - difficult ones like cutting out sugar entirely and becoming absolutely vigilant about not eating dairy, wheat, corn and potatoes. You just don't know how prevalent these ingredients are until you make the choice to eliminate them. This advice basically meant I would need to prepare everything that went in my mouth.

A short time later, in October of 2007, I saw my father's sister, Jayne, at a wedding. It was the first time I had seen her since I was a very young woman, though we had stayed in touch by mail. Her husband, Tommy, had died around the same time as my father. Jayne asked if I would come to her home in Tulsa, Oklahoma to "help her with her boxes." I wasn't exactly sure what she wanted from me, but I made arrangements to visit her in the spring.

At the wedding, she told me the story of Tommy's apparent encounter with my father even as each of them lay dying in separate states. Without prompting, one day late in Tommy's illness, he said to her, "I am sorry your brother died." At that time, Jayne knew, Dad had not yet passed. Jayne and I arrived at this way of making sense of Tommy's comment. Those who are dying, it seems, check out of this world gradually. Perhaps, from time to time, they pass over to that other side and then come back as they prepare for their final transition into death. I've heard bereavement counselors allude to this; it seems to explain why the dying often reach their hands out in front of them, in the air, as if reaching out to someone. Perhaps my uncle and my father crossed paths somewhere in that in-between place. My uncle perceived that my father had actually passed when really he was just "passing though" momentarily at that time. Uncanny. I found a deep grounding in the peaceful knowing that there is somewhere we go when we leave here.

Days before I left for Tulsa, I got word that Aunt Jayne had had a small stroke but was recovering in the hospital. I kept with my plans and saw her as soon as I arrived. She seemed to be in good spirits. Then her friend took me to her house. She had insisted that I stay at her house, drive her car, et cetera. When I got in the house, I struggled to comprehend what I saw. She was not exactly a hoarder, but she was the family historian. She had saved everything of relevance to her own and her husband's families. Her office held an entire wall filled with filing cabinets. Those drawers were all full, so there were stacks and stacks of uncategorized papers and mementoes all over the house. She had asked me there to help her downsize in case she needed to move to a higher level of care in the retirement community where she lived. It was obvious that, whether she moved or returned to this house with in-home care, someone was going to have to get her house in shape. Her friend told me that he and his wife had tried to help her. They had spent an entire afternoon guiding her to decide what to do with a stack of papers he indicated in the corner of the office. The stack was still there. He confirmed they made hardly any progress in those several hours. That was one stack.

I comprehended she was a woman who did not let go of things readily and perhaps had trouble making decisions. Later, doctors determined she had already had several other small strokes. I imagine it was very difficult for her, mentally, to sort through the decision-making process of what to pack and what to throw away. It probably was also difficult emotionally. She had asked for my help. Her friend and his wife had kind of adopted her and Tommy, even before Tommy died. I discovered later that Tommy initiated and pursued this relationship with them, getting their word to watch out for Jayne after he was gone. They had done a lot - taking her to medical appointments, keeping her company, getting groceries for her when that was needed. The organization of the house was a different challenge. They correctly saw the need for a family member to step in. Once again, I saw a task that was mine to do. I had the skill and could make the time.

CHAPTER SEVENTEEN

The Wall

Almost everything will work again if you unplug
it for a few minutes, including you.
~Anne Lamont

I had been experiencing extreme stress before this trip. I still felt unable to will myself to return to the practice of daily meditation for renewal. Without that release, the personal and job stress felt increasingly overwhelming even before I went to Tulsa. My one week trip turned in to three as my aunt recovered and finally came home to an orderly and deep-cleaned home. She was thrilled. At first.

I saw my doctor when I got back from Tulsa. He recommended no activity other than work and the essential activities of living. He believed that my adrenal glands were weakened and would only recover if I eliminated all stress. I followed his advice as best I could. I felt I really had to go back to Tulsa to check on my aunt once more. When I returned three weeks later, I discovered she had realized how much of the "stuff" she was familiar with in her home had been packed away and moved. She was unhappy, perhaps even angry at me, though she never said that. I think she knew my intention was to be of service to her. But it must have been shocking for her to return to a home where things were so different. I felt uncertain of myself and wondered if I had done the right thing for her. I was devastated at not receiving the thanks I thought I deserved for spending all of my vacation time tending to her home so she could live there with her 24/7 caregivers.

We tried to clear this tension between us, but it still felt thick when I left. Talking on the phone quickly became impossible. Her speech was slurred and no one could help me understand what she was trying to say. I told her I loved her. I probably apologized a hundred times for causing her distress. Her friends told her over and over that they would bring from storage anything she wanted. I don't think that was the point. Her "normal" had been disrupted. I imagine she may have felt somewhat violated. Due to the effects of the stroke, she may not even have been able to name the thing she wished was still there, in a familiar stack on the table, or the chair, or the piano, or in that little alcove on the floor.

After that trip, I knew I couldn't travel any more, though I had hoped to return in the summer. I was eventually diagnosed with adrenal fatigue, a condition in which the adrenal glands can no longer produce the levels of cortisol necessary to sustain a body. Fatigue was the primary symptom. I was signed off work for one month, then for another as I struggled to cope with the situation.

Aunt Jayne died that September. In my grief, I eventually realized that her decline and passing all happened the way it needed to happen. Her friend and his wife were there with her and tended to her every need for all those months. He was with her the night before she died; he was the one who asked her if she wanted a feeding tube. He probably held her hand when she decided against it. After months of wrestling with my upset over her displeasure, I realized she needed to be mad at me, not at him. I guess this is just what family does. We care for one another even through the difficult times, allowing ourselves to be mad at each other. My clearing of her home was like pulling off the band-aid. It had to be done, whether she wanted it or not, in order for her healing to progress.

Healing, in this case, did not mean recovery but, rather, a relatively peaceful journey toward her death. My efforts provided her an orderly place that was safe for caregivers to move around in to comfort her in her final days. If she died mad at me, I can live with that. I don't think she did, though. She was a woman who knew the power of Love. They buried her with the quilt she made for her husband and with her favorite little stuffed toy, "Ted Bear."

Her funeral was set for a Wednesday. I couldn't travel to attend it. At the time, I had back pain so severe I could barely navigate to and from the bathroom. With adrenal glands producing only very minimal amounts of cortisol, I was suffering with no ability to put out the fire of inflammation. I got word from Tulsa that I had apparently failed to obtain one necessary signature having to do with her safe deposit boxes. The contents could not be released without my physical presence there. A few weeks after the funeral, my husband travelled with me; I could not have done it alone.

I was able to visit her crypt. My Aunt Jayne, like her mother, was a Christian woman who strived to live a good life. I do believe she forgave me. It did take me a few more weeks to come to a place of peaceful acceptance of her transition and my role in her final days. I was the one who messed with her stuff; I was bound to be the target of her upset. That is why it was mine to do - I was and am emotionally strong enough to survive that. In the end, I am glad she asked me to have that time with her, however troubled, while she was alive.

I turned 53 that November. Often extremely fatigued, my days consisted mostly of lying on the couch. The fatigue was so far beyond the walking-through-water tiredness that comes with depression. This was if-I-don't-lie-down-soon-I'm-going-to-collapse fatigue. It felt like walking through oatmeal. My doctor said my recovery would take time - months and months. I kept hoping I could go back to work; on my best days that seemed possible. On the bad days, though, I couldn't imagine sitting across from a client in need; I felt I had so little to give. I wondered how I would ever feel right again.

My mother had died at age 53 and about five months. Aware of the milestone approaching, I worked hard to keep a positive outlook. I followed the doctor's orders as best I could. I had arrived in this situation by pushing myself way beyond the stopping point. Anyone might think it would be easy to stay home, watch movies, read and cook dinner if I felt up to it. The inactivity was hell for me, though. In addition to my "Type A" personality, the work ethic that I found so attractive in my husband and in his family had propelled me into a continuing desire for activity. I had already worked full-time while going to graduate school with a full load. When I married, I had just kept pushing, to keep up with him, work at my job, care for our home and enjoy being part of a couple. Not working felt like a failure, like I had done something wrong.

Sitting around was not my comfort zone at all. I think it took an entire six months for me to slow down from the warp speed at which I had been living life. Ever so gradually, the trip to the grocery store became a task I could accomplish with ease and plenty of time instead of the hassle and push-push it had been to shop after a full day's work. I noticed how much more pleasant I was with the clerks and I understood that simple fact as a measure of prosperity - feeling confident in having the time to really interact with people instead of rushing through as though others do not exist, do not matter.

In that time of quiet and rest, I pondered, queried and searched to find some new definition of myself. My life had been so full and so complete - great job, fabulous husband, stepchildren, grandkids, wonderful friends and spiritual practices that had nourished me. I felt cut off from all of that. I wasn't even sure if my friends understood my situation. They were all working and I lost touch with many of them for a while. I was just too tired to move at times. It felt like a kind of death. In retrospect I believe part of me was dying, had to die in order for the rest of me to fully come to life. For the time being, though, I felt completely robbed of meaning or purpose to my life. I found great insight in Judith Orloff's book *Positive Energy* which helped me understand that some of my concerns were related to being an Empath, with need for quiet time and energetic protections to recharge after being in the presence of others.

I tried everything else I could think of to heal the adrenal fatigue - Bowen method massage for the pain and acupuncture to try to regain some energy and stamina. I even went several times to Tong Ren sessions, an extremely alternative group healing practice related to acupuncture. Finally, I stopped. Everything. I stopped chasing after healing. I surrendered to the reality that I could not do anything to hurry the process along. I spent most of my time lying down on the couch until I worked through my resistance to staying in bed. I had gotten so caught up in the Do of my career. Now, I was learning to just Be.

I gradually came to spend time in productive activities. In short spurts, I wrote and pursued hobbies like beading and painting to amuse myself. I hired help to keep the house clean because bodily inflammation still flared painfully at unpredictable times. I cooked healthy foods for my husband and me. This became the rhythm of my life - so much slower, calmer and easier than it had been when I was working with people who were in so much pain that it spilled into me.

As the requisite number of months had gone by and I still felt fatigued much of the time, I began searching for additional alternative methods of healing. Dream tending had reawakened my curiosity about shamanistic ways of seeing dis-ease, and I found my way to a shaman for a type of healing called spirit removal. A friend had worked with a shaman whom he recommended with warmth and enthusiasm. I drove the 40 miles to see her in her office even though she often works with people remotely. She is able to see what is true for her clients whether they are seated in front of her or across the planet. I learned how suffering beings (those who have died and left their bodies but have no knowledge of how to travel to the light to enter the world beyond the veil) find refuge in the energetic fields of living beings. The living beings are often exceptionally sensitive to begin with. When stress comes, the energetic field of the living being develops a fissure or crack which opens the field to allow the suffering being to enter and stay there, siphoning energy from the living host.

In my first session, the shaman worked to remove six suffering beings. From a mild trance state, I could sense the beings as they appeared, one at a time. I suspect the shaman had a more immediately clear understanding of who they were, but she listened as I struggled to describe them a little. It was like feeling around for something in the dark, knowing where my hand is in space, but not knowing where anything else really is. Images came in snippets, like little dreams. She confirmed my impressions and, each time, had me ask the being who had loved them on this plane. That person, then, came from the other side to our edge of the tunnel of light and beckoned the being home. The shaman then worked in silence to complete some aspects of the healing which she did not explain to me except to say that she was ensuring the final and total entrance of that being into the light.

Despite what I had read, I went into this experience feeling very skeptical. I didn't really believe any great change would come from it. But it was something else to try when I had tried everything. So I took the risk of spending money for perhaps no benefit. (One thing I had learned in those seminars years before is, when in doubt, take action and the universe will provide feedback.)

The shaman told me about one of the beings who had died in a fistfight when he fell over a 30 foot wall and landed on his neck. There were other stories – one for each being – as well. The first thing I noticed at the end of the session, though, was a remarkable release of the chronic pain in my neck and shoulders. Over the coming days and weeks, I did begin to notice a greater sense of well-being and a subtle shift to greater and greater energy. She told me that the beings only surface during this type of shamanic treatment when the time is correct for that to happen. It struck me as a pretty good pitch for ongoing business, but I tried to let go of that thought quickly to focus instead on the amazing results I had gotten from her work.

About two years later, I did contact her again and had a remote session this time because, ironically, she had moved to New Orleans.

I told her I had a strong sense that my father may have landed in my field when he died. She said this was unlikely but she would take a look. She sent me instructions on how to participate in the session when she was 1500 miles away. Then she called me on the phone to follow up a few minutes after it was over. She confirmed that she had removed my father and sent him on his way into the light, his mother greeting him in the tunnel. If I had not already had a powerful and very helpful experience with her shamanic healing techniques, I might have dismissed this. It was after that session, though, that I began to feel a resurgence of energy – both physical and mental. I remembered with a certain sad but surrendered smile how tiring "my grief" over my father had been. I wondered how I would have experienced the aftermath of his passing differently if I had known to tell him that night in my living room to go to the light, to find the one who had loved him most dearly on this earth and to go with her to that place of eternal love.

CHAPTER EIGHTEEN

Reckoning

*You are a drop of the divine. Know this and
then wait. Have patience. Lean on the divine
and amazing things will come to you.*
~Yogi Bhajan

Still on a medical leave, I spent weeks struggling with a decision to leave the job I had loved so much. Leaving the job might also mean leaving my career. Arriving at that decision was becoming a journey in itself.

In February of 2009, I joined a Dream Tending group. I had never before been part of a dream group. My studies of Art Therapy and other forms of psychological depth work had gifted me with a fascination and respect for unconscious material rising to the level of conscious recognition in artwork, automatic writing and dreams and I was eager to explore.

This group consisted of only therapists. It seemed like a good way to mine my subconscious for guidance about how to heal and how to find clarity regarding the best next step in my life. Eight of us gathered on alternate Thursday mornings to enter into our dream lives together with the goal of more fully understanding the wisdom and symbols therein. Unlike dream interpretation, Dream Tending holds the dreamer at the center of understanding the dream. Our wise and experienced group leader would ask us questions to guide us to greater understanding of the dream and why it came to us at the particular time it did. Group members supported the process and offered insights based on our own projections. Owning my projections into the dreams of others was a powerful process that opened me to new revelations about myself and my motivations.

I was already anticipating passing through the age my mother had been when she died. That would occur in April of that year. I predicted this as a final milestone of my healing from her suicide death. I had no idea what moving through that invisible threshold would entail. As I approached it, however, I was well aware that my maternal grandmother had lived only to age 51. If my intuition about my mother was correct, then she spent the last two years of her life feeling that she did not deserve to live longer than her mother had. That was clearly a different kind of misery than I was experiencing myself. I continue to express my gratitude that I do not have bipolar disease, which often appears to have a genetic link. Although I was still having times of despair regarding my health and my situation, these were moments in the day, not weeks at a time. Yet I found myself stuck in a place in my life that did not seem to be allowing me to move forward in the direction I wanted to go

The symptoms of adrenal fatigue are very much like chronic fatigue syndrome. At times, I felt that if I didn't lie down right away, I would just collapse. Testing of the adrenal glands via mainstream medicine techniques showed no apparent pathology in my adrenal gland: I did not have Addison's disease, also known as hypoadrenia - a condition typically treated with regular doses of synthetic corticosteroids.[127] However, saliva testing of my cortisol levels indicated my adrenal glands were under-functioning to the extreme, with no spike in the morning to wake me up and an unusual increase in the evening level. For me, this meant that after a day of struggling against exhaustion to get anything done, I would get to bed at night, only to feel suddenly wide awake.

According to Wikipedia: "Cortisol is a steroid hormone ... it is released in response to stress and low blood glucose concentration. It functions to increase blood sugar through gluconeogenesis, to suppress the immune system, and to aid in the metabolism of fat, protein, and carbohydrate. It also decreases bone formation."[128]

I came to think of cortisol as my body's fire extinguisher, rushing in to soothe stress – both mental and physical. With only very low levels, every minor pain in my body became more intense. I struggled with severe lower back pain for four months. With even a small degree of psychological stress, my thinking turned clouded and confused. I could barely track what I read. Because I believe that nothing happens by accident, I asked God for guidance about what I needed to learn or experience from this situation in order to move beyond it, into my complete recovery from it. I wanted an answer immediately. It did not come. Without answers, I learned to live in the question and soon realized that there were deeper lessons and other roads for me to travel to find my way back to the energy and capability I had operated from in the past. My deepest lesson was to learn to trust that I was already moving in the direction of my highest good, even when I couldn't see any possible way to get there from where I was.

As I moved through physical pain every day, I spent hour after hour lying in bed, doing practically nothing. I surprised myself at how successfully I held at bay the despair that came with the inactivity. Yet I couldn't help reviewing the dreaded memories of my mother sleeping her life away, often drunk to some degree and always sedated on psychotropic medications. I fought against the cognitive distortion that I was becoming her. I reminded myself that I was not using substances to numb myself; I was not even seeking pharmaceutical pain relievers and was, instead, following excellent alternative medical advice in order to get well. I relied on these distinctions between us and also came to realize that they were remnants of the judgments I had held on her since I was young.

I had hoped that this milestone of moving through the age she was at her passing would be a little speed bump on my road into late middle age. The weeks prior to it, though, plunged me into issues I thought I had resolved long before. I delved again into those murky waters of what had been between us. I came to comprehend my mother's pain in a much different way. My ponderings included the question of what my mother experienced in the weeks and months prior to her fateful decision. I wondered if she had experienced anything like this fatigue. Then I recalled that she had once told me that if she'd had her life to do over again, she would have studied medicine, with special focus on the endocrine system. I now suspect she had discussions with her psychiatrist about the endocrine system. My mother was in menopause before the widespread use of hormone replacement therapy, though she may have benefitted from early versions of that. In addition to her other sources of misery, she may have been having hot flashes, foggy thinking and sleep disruption on top of the sleep disorder that alcohol abuse usually brings about. She certainly was not very active in the years before she died. She hardly left her bedroom. I had attributed all of this to alcohol abuse alone. I wondered if she had possibly suffered from endocrine imbalances as well.

This question led me to the realization that I had never fully grasped what life was like for her. Some of these things she would have been reluctant to discuss with her child. But I wonder if she held back on some of the other things simply because I had judged her so harshly that I was not really a safe audience. So, now I had to face up to how judgmental and unkind I had been to her. Having completed the long journey of forgiving *her* for her final act of self-destruction that had caused me so much pain, I finally faced the glaring reality that I now needed to ask her to forgive *me*.

Although I did love my mother, I had rejected her as any kind of a role model from my mid-teens forward. She became my anti-role model. From the time of my spiritual awakening at One Seminar, lying on that floor, feeling my heart beat, I had set out to live my life in a way diametrically opposed to hers. In this way, I hoped to avoid the pitfalls that had captured her - resentments about the past she could not change, alcoholism, the lack of awareness of how to move through pain instead of holding on, numbing and her eventual complete self-destruction.

The decision I made in my mid-twenties – that my life was not going to blindly follow my mother's – was and still is my Alchemical Inheritance. I know I came to this planet with a choice to suffer the fates of my ancestors or to take charge and transform my life. My mother and her mother came from families with great wealth, as I did also. Watching the wealth in my family slowly erode into nothing was the best thing that ever could have happened to me. The wealth itself became like an addictive substance. As long as the money was in the family, family relied on it. I had no incentive to find my skill and my passion. That just was not part of the value system in which I had been raised, much to the detriment of my siblings and me. I had no idea of what it meant to *get* to work at something that gave me joy. Searching and finding that in myself moved me toward the my best possible life, finding meaningful ways to contribute to society, accepting with grace and joy all that is mine to do.

With this awareness, I cried more tears and released an entire new layer of grief. I confronted unwanted aspects of myself – the rough edges – and worked to soften my judgments of others in general. When we are busy in our daily lives, with our minds constantly working to discern friend from foe, good from bad, helpful from hurtful, we often don't realize we are judging and don't understand the violence of judgment. While it may not appear to be physically violent to harbor judgmental thoughts, a little contemplation will usually cause a person to realize that harboring such thoughts does do harm. Such thoughts held in mind obviously lead to negative thinking and the resulting dysphoria. Those, in turn, become a nursery for regret, resentment and vengeance. Harder to quantify, though, is how such thoughts may eventually damage the physical integrity of the body. Thoughts are the earliest energetic signature of what may become actions. Unkind thoughts breed unkind actions and then may even breed further unkindness.

As I renewed my vigilance to reduce the harmful content of some of my thoughts, I felt my soul softening. This became a practical experience of the truth that the peace we seek in the outer world has to begin within each of us. As I worked through a variety of processes to seek and achieve forgiveness of myself and others, I had several cathartic experiences of graceful release of judgment. I have no doubt that from somewhere across the ethers, the spiritual essence of my mother gifted me with the clear and comforting awareness of complete forgiveness from her. It washed over me, filling me with an integrated sense of wholeness. I remember a moment in which I was bathed in a love so big and encompassing that it made the long journey so worth it. After that, I came to see my mother, once again, as the smiling, golden-haired woman that she had been when she sang with us in the car on the way home from the ranch. In my mind, now, she is always smiling.

Counselors would say that I had simply held judgment on myself and through those processes, was able to release it. Yes, that too. It is my belief that these matters of the soul transcend time and space and that our attainment of the peace of forgiveness comes from somewhere far beyond the reaches of rational thought. Either way, healing is the result.

When the actual time of the milestone arrived in April, I crossed over it without much turmoil. This was like the anticipation of the anniversary of a loved one's death. It's the lead-up that counts - our attitude and expectation of how it will come to pass. The way we *approach* the date is often what heals the heart or, at least, spurs us on to feel the pain and this, in turn, can reduce the pain little by little. Such is the work of grieving.

In June of that year, about three months after the milestone, I dreamed a dream that I titled *Liquefaction*.

In the dream, I see a mother pleading to be allowed to remain in an area where liquefaction (the liquefying of the soil due to seismic forces) is predicted with certainty in the very near future - the next few days. I am an observer, hovering in the air, out over the water, looking at the coast line. From that distance and perspective, I see a deep cleft on the coastline below her location. It is easy to discern from the steepness of the cleft that the water becomes very deep, very fast. Still in the dream but now on the land and facing the mother, I witness her religious fervor about wanting to stay where she is for the event. There is a hint that she wants her child to be with her for the experience and this is the primary source of controversy and objection to her plan. I make eye contact with her as she states her case. I continue to observe this scene and come to know that the child is now safe, separated from the mother. I see the liquefaction take place. I am still watching as the mother becomes one with the earth as it liquefies and merges with the sea. The child is safe.

This entire book is encapsulated in this dream. In my waking state, I chose to describe the coastline as a "cleft." It is such a descriptive word and, in that sleepy moment of writing, I did not yet realize the close tie to the cleft of my palate at the time of my birth. The Mother figure is one of several key figures in Carl Jung's Analytical Psychology, one foundation of this approach to dream work. Psychology teaches about individuation – the process of maturation whereby an infant moves from complete connection to the mother (in the womb) through various stages of increasing autonomy, finally arriving at adulthood and (theoretically) complete autonomy and independence from the mother.

The mother in my dream is pleading to be released from her earthly, physical body. When that happens, it is evident that she will fall into very deep water – a symbol of the emotional realm and the collective unconscious. In the dream, I am the observer and know I cannot stop her. I am simply a witness. Even though I question her choice, it is hers, not mine, to make. I am also the child who does not go with her, as much as the mother may want her to. The child has individuated physically, psychologically but, especially, spiritually. The child knows that mother has to go as much as the child knows the child has to *not* go.

For me, the certainty of the prediction of *Liquefaction* reflects the destined outcome of my mother's response to her mother's murder. It seems to reflect that all occurs in divine order, according to a plan that is far beyond our own making. The mother in my dream is completely peaceful with making the transition of becoming one with the earth. Like the child in the dream, I have, in my waking life, arrived at that place of complete acceptance of her life and her death - just as they were.

My life has unfolded in series of seven-year periods. It is no surprise to me that it took seven years for me to fully recover from adrenal fatigue and find my way into a more balanced life. I released the notion of returning to the stressful world of corporate mental health and medicine in exchange for a large paycheck. I let go of my career by moving into semi-retirement with my husband as I lead Dream Tending groups and occasionally see clients for coaching and hypnotherapy.

I have found my way back into rhythms of living that incorporate daily self-care in the form of meditation, nourishment, exercise, rest and recreation. My minister, Reverend Michael Moran, who was preparing to retire during this time of my uncertainty, gifted me with a bit of wisdom by quoting Lao Tsu: "Happy is the one who has determined how much is enough."

CHAPTER NINETEEN

Awakening

"Real isn't how you were made," said the Skin Horse.
"It's a thing that happens to you. When a child loves
you for a long, long time, not just to play with, but
REALLY loves you, then you become Real."
~Margery Williams

Only recently have I come to realize how few years there were between Nana's death and my grade-school years. For those first 8 to 10 years of my life, my mother was caught - or stuck - in her grieving process. She hadn't yet really allowed herself to feel all of the feelings of grief - the intense sadness along with the conflicted feelings of relief that Washburn's threats had come to an end. The anger, or more accurately, *rage* over the brutality of the slaying must have roiled within her still. Like many people, she numbed that pain with alcohol and probably had no idea at the time that her reliance would become a dependence and that dependence would be her undoing. I imagine that with every drink she drifted farther and farther from the aspects of her life that (I hope) had given her joy - her husband and children.

As an adult, I struggled to heal from this sense of abandonment. I came to understand it in the context of codependence, a symptom that developed in me because my mother was more involved with alcohol than with her children. I developed into a person with a belief that I was responsible for others and was somehow required and able to intervene and control their lives for them. I did my time in Al-Anon and came to the liberating realization that I am only responsible for myself. Yet, at another level, I have come to believe that there was a higher, even divine, purpose for my relationship with my mother. From a spiritual perspective, unbound by the restrictions of linear time, I came to understand a deeper dance between us that may have explained my behavior as a child.

I think I was meant to be the child of my mother. I believe I was born to her partly so I could help her heal and partly so she could lead me to my own healing. This healing activity was not literal though, not meant to be the result of my actions or conversations with her. Rather, it provided a spiritual connection that held the opportunity for us to see ourselves more clearly, each in the mirror of the other. Her actions and choices would usher in my life's greatest challenge – healing from her absence in my life and leaving behind my misplaced belief that I am responsible for the actions and feelings of others. In a spiritual sense, I think we are all thrown together in our wonderfully varied human bodies by seemingly random genetics but also through a mystical process of selection that allows each of us to live our lives in the company of others who cause us to confront different aspects of ourselves and thereby, grow our souls.

Although it took me seven long years to begin to resolve my grief over her passing, some other remaining wounds of my childhood were mostly healed at the same time. That process necessitated my confronting the realities of her alcoholism and its impact on my personality. Then I set about doing the difficult work of reshaping who I am. I believe that in healing my wounded heart on this plane, *her* heart and soul are healed on the plane where she continues to exist - where we all exist for all time. In fact, most of the healing of my relationship with my mother has come since her death. This dance of life ends in its present form when one of us dies, but in another form or in another dimension, the dance goes on. The relationship continues and the healing can too, if we pursue that. The relationship continues for as long as we interact with our memories and develop our understanding of who that person was and why it came to be that we were together on this planet for a time.

My training as a psychotherapist taught me to both look for and work from the power of metaphor in human experience. A child suffering from anxiety due to repeated lice infections may not be able to talk about lice or bugs, but can draw a vivid depiction of the conquering of aliens invading the planet. A middle-aged man, forced into retirement due to a chronic but not yet life-threatening illness may have suicidal thoughts before (and unless) he comes to realize that it is not his life that must end, but only the life he once knew.

I believe this is the overarching explanation of why my mother chose to end her life. She had suffered long and hard, to be sure. Yet, just prior to her death, she discovered a potential road map out of her suffering through the Alcoholics Anonymous program. It would not have unfolded as a quick and easy solution - far from it. She could have claimed the road map and, yes, she could have created a support team for a long journey with many difficult climbs and very rocky roads along the way. Of course the promise of stunning vistas on the way was implied, if only she had travelled a little farther down that road.

Finding sobriety means losing most of what has been known territory in the landscapes of a person's life - personality, values, expectations and ways of interacting with others, especially loved ones. I believe the fatal flaw for my mother was that she could not see herself being anything *more* - more clear, more joyful, more empowered, more at peace. Absent that vision, the finality of actual, physical death became her only option.

Sobriety, via the Twelve Steps of Alcoholics Anonymous, would have demanded that she not only accept herself as she was but also that she genuinely come to love herself despite her faults, judgments and failures. She would have had to forgive not only those who had wronged her but, more importantly, to forgive herself. Just like the birthing process, this kind of re-birthing process carries with it inherent risks and dangers as well as the miraculous promise of new life.

I know in the depths of me that my mother was aware of having outlived her own mother. I imagine this gnawed at her and kept her stuck, not knowing how to live longer than her mother and, likely, not feeling she deserved to thrive in those extra years. So my mother succumbed to the risks before she could grab on to the promise: joy in her heart as the reward for hard work achieved at great personal sacrifice over a long period of time.

Yet, part of me wonders still if her manner of death was simply "written" in her book of life or her Akashic record or someplace within her where her fate was stored. I have wondered if she always knew she would die by suicide and that is why she told me about the gardener who lit himself on fire. I am sure that doctors drilled into her the responsibility she had to raise all of her children. Perhaps she was preparing me for life and for her death.

My resistance to becoming like my mother funded my ability to develop myself into a capable person and a skilled professional counselor. I am grateful for that. I went back into counseling, this time with a most enlightened counselor, Stephen Bryant Walker, Stephen is also a Buddhist monk, known as Lama Jinpa. That Buddhist perspective helped me to see this resistance within me as a polarity and not an ideal state of being. Not wanting to become my mother, I had become opposite her and that had created a longstanding tension inside of me. In order to find an enduring peace within, I had some more work to do. I learned to go into meditation and hold, simultaneously, that resistance along with my emerging acceptance of all that is. As those two polarities came closer together in my time sitting with them, the tension in my life began to lessen and eventually resolve. I was finding a place of integration. I now feel my life is funded from a much more vital, original source, a life force which I cultivate and deepen in my frequent meditations.

I have outlived my mother. It is a strange feeling to have no understanding of how my mother was at the age I am now. How would she have looked if she had taken charge of her health? How would she have dealt with turning 60 or 70? How could she have come to rely on her faith to guide her and support her?

Fortunately I have chosen well the other role models in my life. Women ministers and especially my husband's mother, Pauline, have all guided me in the gentle way of simply being the capable and compassionate people they are or were. The journey up this mountain has been long and, at times, incredibly difficult. But the vista from here is expansive, the air clear and soothing and the horizons broad and compelling. My role models also come in the less tangible forms of dream imagery and belief in higher powers supporting me on my continuing journey to develop aspects within me that are capable of serving the highest good for all and for our planet.

I pledge to do my best.

Epilogue

The journey of a thousand miles begins with a single step.
~Lao-Tsu

I can't believe how long it took. All those years just to come to the awareness that my mother actually was *standing* in front of that mirror just before she died; and all of those years to come to the awareness that I may have been molested. My own subconscious mind held that information just below the level of my conscious awareness in order to protect me from content too overwhelming for me at the time. Then, when I was ready, it also brought me a dream (*Liquefaction*) signaling the completion of my individuation from my mother. By then, I was over 50 years old. The journey takes as long as it takes.

As a very young child, the first book that captured my attention was *Harold and the Purple Crayon*. I loved to follow the adventures of Harold. In easy words and simple, striking line drawings, he creates a picture of each thing he will next encounter as he moves forward into his story. He encounters many joys and great beauty as well as monsters and fears along the way, but there is always a vision in his mind that addresses current circumstances to successfully move him beyond his own limitations.

Given the powerful role imagery has played in my journey - from treasure mapping to vision boards to dream tending and beyond - it is simply perfect to now recall that Harold was my first inspiration.

It seems I had within me all that I needed for life from the start. It was there in that little book. Then I forgot.

And isn't that true for all of us? It seems to be the nature of living our lives that we come here from God, filled with infinite knowledge and perfection. Then we forget. We forget who we are and why we have come. We forget precisely so we can experience the experience of figuring it all out again. We just have to be awake.

It is my deepest desire that *Alchemical Inheritance* has awakened and inspired you to pursue your continuing healing and self-development in places you may have missed. In that way, you are invited to move beyond whatever may be holding you back from the most empowered and enlightened expression of who you are.

As we do our work, we also need others around us to remind us of our gifts and our missions. Please surround yourself with others who share your vision for yourself. These great souls show up in all kinds of places, from churches and 12-step meetings to schools, service clubs, gyms and yoga classes. They may even be waiting at the bus stop.

If needed, find a doctor for a correct diagnosis of any mental health concerns and then get to a counselor who hears your need and comprehends your journey. With national health care now so available, part of being a good citizen is doing this healing work so that your unique contribution can impact our world for the better. And don't stop with traditional counseling services. Become a gourmet of personal development. (Oprah has shown us the way!)

Choose carefully the professionals you hire to guide you. Interview them to find out if they have climbed the mountains that you are facing, or at least have helped others climb them. The ones I have climbed are called Abandonment, Grief, Suicide of a Parent, Substance Abuse, Spiritual Awakening, Empowerment, Abundance and the Value of Service to Others. The paradox here is most counselors are trained to avoid self-disclosure unless it is in the express interest of the client. Often, counselors don't openly share their personal journeys but I believe clients have a right to ask.

Finally, we can punctuate our own progress by giving away what we have found. Some of us have careers where we serve others. Others of us find other ways to give back. We all can give in a multitude of tiny, unrecognized and perhaps even unnoticed ways. Consider the kindness involved in wiping the wet countertop after you wash up in a public restroom. Perhaps no one is there to notice it. The next person coming in may very well just expect the countertop to be dry and clean. But *you* will know in that tiny way you contributed to making the world a better place. From such tiny acts, a great wellspring of goodwill can grow.

I know I am powerless to stop the terror and violence that are erupting all too frequently in our world now, but I can be Peace in my own mind, in my own heart, in my family and in my community.

We all can.

Tess Keehn, M.S., C.H.T.
AlchemicalInheritance@gmail.com

Appendix A
Harris Family History

We are born at a given moment, in a given place and,
like vintage years of wine, we have the qualities of the
year and of the season of which we are born.
~Carl Jung

My maternal aunt, Sadie Gwin Blackburn, wrote the following summary of the Harris family ancestry and entry into Texas in the early 19th Century. With gratitude for her hours of research, I quote her work in italics, tying it together with my own understanding of our family's ancestry.

"Gonzales became a gathering place for Texas fighting men during the early part of the Texas Revolution since nearby San Antonio was the principal center of government in Texas and the scene of early clashes. Thirty men of Gonzales made their way through the Mexican forces surrounding the Alamo in 1836 to join the defending Texans and died in that famous battle. Outnumbered by thousands of Mexican soldiers, the few hundred Texans were overcome and slaughtered by Santa Anna's orders. The only survivors were Mrs. Susannah Dickerson, her baby girl, and two black servant men. Arriving at Gonzales the next day, they delivered Santa Anna's message to Sam Houston, who had arrived from Washington-on-the-Brazos, having been appointed to lead the Texas forces gathering there. The message was clear: Anyone opposing him would suffer the same fate as the defenders of the Alamo, death with no quarter. There were thirty new widows in Gonzales that day, and Houston sent his soldiers to gather up all the widows and

children and prepare to take them along with the army as it marched east across Texas. He included Mrs. Gilliam in this group of widows. Lt. Votaw helped the Gilliams pack up to accompany the march of the Texas Army across Texas. The oldest son, Berry, rode behind the lieutenant on his horse. Leasel drove a wagon in which Barbara Gilliam had hastily piled as many of the family's belongings as possible, since general Houston had given orders that Gonzales was to be burned in order to prevent Santa Anna from gaining any supplies or shelter during the coming conflict. Families with their wagons camped with the Army as it moved across Texas, finally arriving at the San Jacinto River.

"Houston hoped to be joined by Fannin and his men from Goliad but sadly received news a few days later of the Goliad Massacre. Houston continued his eastward march, keeping his men safely north of the Brazos River, which was in flood and prevented the superior Mexican force from attacking the smaller Texas army. As they approached the San Jacinto River, a Mexican messenger was captured whose papers revealed that Santa Anna had separated a small contingent from his main force in order to go to Harrisburg, where he was told that the officers of the newly-formed Texas government were staying. He found buildings burning, all people gone but learned they had fled to Morgan's Point. Arriving there, he discovered them already launched in a boat for Galveston. Turning his forces back north toward the San Jacinto River, he found that Sam Houston had crossed Buffalo Bayou and camped with his men, now numbering close to the same number as the Mexicans with Santa Anna. Many of the families from Gonzales were still with the Texian Army, including the Gilliams, and were camped nearby. The Gilliams remained on their point of land where the bayou emptied into the San Jacinto River, heard the battle, and the next day were present when the captured Santa Anna was brought before Sam Houston.

"The defeat and capture of Santa Anna allowed the establishment of the independent Republic of Texas and the later admission of this Republic as a state into the United States in 1845. Offers by the United States to pay Mexico, which had never recognized Texas' independence, for the territory were refused, and the Mexican War ensued in 1848-49. In the initial stages of the War, General Zachary Taylor could not legally use the state militia but he could include informal groups of volunteers such as the Texas Rangers.

"Barbara Gilliam had married Lt. Votaw after the Texas Revolution despite the fact that Votaw was much younger than Barbara, actually only a little older than Leasel. Leasel was seventeen when Barbara died and he left home to join the Texas Rangers. He was a friend of Henry McCullough's son Ben, and both young men fought in McCullough's Rangers during the Mexican War. After the war, on the way home from Mexico, the young men gathered a herd of wild horses. These horses gave Leasel his start at ranching on the San Marcos River property that his stepfather Gilliam had claimed for him. For a period of time, he realized additional income by driving a delivery ox cart for the U. S. Army as they established forts across the new addition to the United States.

"Living in San Antonio, he met and married Martha Isabelle McKenzie on June 18, 1851."

Martha Harris' story is interesting in its own right. She was born in 1830 and my Aunt Sadie Gwin has researched her coming to Texas as well:

"Martha Isabelle McKenzie was the third child of Joseph Milton McKenzie and Virginia Bracher Higginbotham McKenzie. ... The McKenzies lived near Nashville, Tennessee, and Martha Isabelle attended private school in that city. Upon the initiative of her father's brother, the two McKenzie families decided to come to Texas. ... They came down the Mississippi with a large group coming to settle in the new Mexican province which had been assured self-government under the 1824 Constitution. They took another ship from New Orleans, which was unfortunately wrecked as they tried to enter harbor at the Colorado River. It was quite close to shore, however, so they were able to recover most of their belongings and make camp along the seashore. In a very short time, however, Karankawa Indians discovered the party and made an attack. Some were lost, but quite a few were able to launch the lifeboats which had been salvaged from the ship, row out into the bay and remain there until the Indians finished looting their belongings and went away. After this incident, the group made its way up the river to San Antonio where they established residence, later moving to Gonzales County. Martha Isabelle married Leasel Bobo Harris on June 18, 1851, in San Antonio, Texas. This marriage produced eight children: Walter Clifton, Eliza Adeline, Clara, William Wayne, Nancy, Frank, Ralph Henry, and Mary. Walter married

Juanita (Barilla), Eliza Adeline married John Slaughter, Clara and William remained unmarried, Nancy married Eugene Cartledge, Frank married Lulu Jones, Ralph married Sadie Ledyard Gwin, and Mary (Mollie) married William F. Childress. Martha Harris insisted that her children return to Nashville to attend the same school she had attended as a young girl. Both Frank and Ralph attended the University of Missouri, and Ralph received his degree in Business Administration."

After his marriage to Martha, *"Leasel Harris's ranching business prospered. Although his largest ranch property was near Pleasanton, he leased other property and enlarged his operations.*

"During the Civil War, Leasel Harris was made a Colonel in the Texas Rangers and charged with the defense of San Antonio, should the Union forces ever invade Texas. After the War, from a desire to provide for his children's future, he sold his east Texas ranch in 1872, left the women in San Antonio, and took his three sons and a son-in-law to the western reaches of Bexar County. (Later on, Tom Green and Coke Counties were carved out of the western reaches of Bexar County.) The four men claimed and homesteaded land in the Colorado River Valley north of San Angelo. After the period of three years required to accomplish homestead claims, Leasel built a house in San Angelo and brought the rest of the family to West Texas. With three friends, he opened the first bank in San Angelo, the Concho Bank, later named the First National Bank."

In the 1870s, the Western reaches of Bexar county included Fort Concho, located in proximity to the Concho and Colorado Rivers. Water was (and is) more and more scarce as you traveled farther and farther west in Texas. The rivers were probably only partially navigable but they provided much needed water, brackish as it may have been, throughout the region. Near the Fort, the town of Ben Ficklin supplied the Fort and civilians with goods and most services. Some services weren't available there, however, so the men stationed at the Fort (and probably many others) went to nearby Saint Angelus for their recreation—drinking, gambling and working girls. At some point, the entire town of Ben Ficklin went up in smoke, so the residents cleaned up Saint Angelus and renamed it San Angelo. There is still a Ben Ficklin road outside of San Angelo. I remember riding across its low water crossing, seeing the eddies and whirlpools of the creek and dreaming vividly of them that night. Water being representative of our unconscious, I marvel that those images visited my dreams and live in my awareness still.

The frontier was moving farther west and Fort Concho was set for closure. To protect the area and maintain the Anglo presence, the U.S. government offered land to male homesteaders. That was how Leasel - now known as L.B. - along with his sons and son-in-law, staked their claims to the ranch land where my Nana lived in 1955. With their wives and sisters in San Antonio, L.B. and the other young men each earned one additional section (640 acres) by living on the land for three years. I am uncertain of the total acreage of their combined holdings but my mother used to say that the family ranchland at one time comprised the whole valley that came into view as you drove north from San Angelo toward Robert Lee over some hills in Coke County locally known as "The Divide."

These were adventurous souls living on the edge of America in the late 1800s. Although the region has dried up a little bit every year since then, at the time it was relatively lush prairie land southeast of Abilene, Texas. Long low mountains with mostly flat tops make the area look like what many people imagine when they think of Texas--big skies, expansive views, sparse vegetation reminiscent of John Ford's Western movies.

Homes were built and the women and children were brought out from San Antonio. L.B.'s son, William Wayne Harris, had died when he was thrown from a horse during a roundup. I believe this was before the West Texas land was claimed. But the other sons married, had their own children, and participated in the business and civic development of San Angelo. Ranching was lucrative and old L.B., it seems, got tired of riding all the way to the bank in San Antonio with the proceeds of his ranching concerns. So he and his friends opened the first local bank that later became the First National Bank of San Angelo.

The land that L.B. and his partners laid claim to had previously been open prairie. With no barriers between Mexico and Kansas, many were accustomed to herding cattle all the way to market in Kansas City. When L.B began to build fences some objections were raised. Custom had it that grazing was done freely, with animals roaming around the entire area. But L.B. Harris likely wanted that grassland for his own cattle. At some point he received a load of fence posts and wire, delivered by railroad. I imagine he had waited a long time for the supplies to arrive. In the black of night some of his neighbors took those posts and piled them up with wire on top or underneath and set fire to the whole pile. This was a significant event in the so-called "Fence Wars" in Coke County. My father tells me a historical marker commemorates the event somewhere in the county. He also said that sometime—probably in the 1960s—my Great Aunt Gwin (Nana's sister) was invited to the dedication of the marker. She declined, suggesting that maybe the descendants of the vandals that destroyed old L.B.'s property might want to show up! I guess she was quite a character but I remember her as a very proper, distinctive woman.

L.B. Harris died in 1906. Someone who actually knew him told my aunt how scary L.B. was, since he persisted in wearing his six shooters long after settlement and civilization had eradicated the need for constant personal protection. I guess if you had lived your life carrying gold to San Antonio, some habits just stuck with you. My mother used to tell a story about one of our ancestors who drank too much and gambled away the family land holdings one night, only to win them back the next night. Who knows if it's true, but I wonder if that was old L.B.

L.B.'s oldest son, Walter, died in his forties and is buried in San Angelo. A small gravestone next to his reads, "Juanita Barilla Wife of Walter Harris 1864 – 1951." She married him but did not take his name. I seem to recall a Mexican custom of woman's surnames being retained after marriage or at least combined with the husband's name. This is a little reminder of the reality that Anglos were settling land that had previously belonged to Mexicans. I am just a little proud that my ancestor was willing to marry in to the local Mexican heritage there. The relatively smaller size of her gravestone seems to telegraph the differences in values and, perhaps, a certain lack of acceptance of her as a family member. But I am only presuming to understand a relationship that was buried without elaboration. An infant gravestone is nearby. I'm sure that branch of the family tree has its own sad stories.

Ralph Harris and his younger brother, Frank Harris, were better known to my aunt and my mother. The two men were grandfather and great uncle (respectively) to my mother, Helen and her sister, Sadie Gwin.

Ralph Henry Harris was L.B. and Martha's seventh child and fourth son. He was born in 1868 in San Antonio. He had the college experience outlined above and then took the offer his father had made to all of the sons--the right to raise cattle on the family property north of San Angelo if each worked to purchase his own herd of cattle. Ralph rode a cattle drive to Kansas City and spent $10,000. on a herd that he brought back. That gave him his start. He most likely rode the Goodnight Trail that ran right through the Harris family property—or at least had run through there before the fences were built. Ralph was 32 when he married Sadie (Ledyard) Gwin from Mobile, Alabama in 1900. She was 26 on her December wedding day in San Angelo. A young woman with so much of her life ahead of her was living on the leading edge of a whole new century.

Ralph and Frank formed a partnership to raise cattle on the family land. They built houses next to each other in San Angelo on the street where their parents lived that came to be called Harris Avenue. Later in life, Ralph and Sadie built a large home several blocks from their earlier home--on the edge of downtown San Angelo, at the corner of Beauregard and Koenigheim.

The couple helped establish and were active in the Episcopal Church on Harris Avenue. Ralph and Frank's families stayed closely connected. They celebrated Christmas together every year with Frank, because he was older, hosting Christmas morning and Ralph and Sadie hosting Christmas Eve. My Aunt Sadie Gwin remembers the brothers' partnership from when she was a little girl. My mother, Helen, used to tell stories about large family gatherings as well.

Three years after her wedding in 1900, Sadie (Gwin) Harris gave birth to my grandmother, Helen Harris. The next child to come along was Ralph, Jr., known as "Buddy." Then came Gwin (my great aunt) and the second son, Ledyard, was the youngest. My mother told us how she used to taunt and tease her Uncle Ledyard. When, as a young child, she learned that every fourth child born in the world was a Chinaman, she would call out, "Ledyard is a Chinaman!" and then run as fast as she could to hide under the front porch before he got to her. The way she told it, Ledyard was severely annoyed by this. I imagine though, that he was just a playful uncle, indulging his niece in a game of chase.

The Harris brothers ranched that land in partnership all of their lives. They employed a fair number of people on the ranches and a small town grew up on the Colorado River in the midst of their property to serve the needs of the ranch hands and their families. The brothers named the town after the man they most admired--Robert E. Lee. Robert Lee became the county seat when Coke County was carved out of the original Bexar County.

I never knew my great-grandmother, Sadie Gwin Harris. I held an unfair view of "Gran" in my childhood, seeing her as a snobby socialite. But I came to understand more about her through a tattered copy of a newspaper article all about the 20th Century Club, a social organization that she joined in its infancy and helped support throughout her life, forming deep friendships and sharing life's joys and tragedies with other women along the way. Now I see her more simply as a young woman in a dusty cow town on the Texas prairie, just doing her best to find enjoyment in a routine sort of life. She became a woman of privilege, thanks to the success of her ranching. That success may have been due to a common practice of overgrazing the land. Perhaps history romanticizes the pioneers that claimed manifest destiny for all of us that followed. Perhaps history tends to forget that they were seekers of opportunity as well as adventurers.

My Gran, Mrs. Ralph Harris, was well known in the San Angelo community. She is pictured at age 76 or so, on the society page of the San Angelo Standard Times on January 11th, 1951, in a photo that marks the Golden Anniversary of the 20th Century Club. She is also pictured at the bottom of the page as the young bride who joined her life-long friend, Mrs. W.A. Guthrie, in being the first two inducted into membership during 1902. The club was dedicated to amusement and entertainment through games and Mrs. Ralph Harris (Sadie Gwin Harris) is remembered for throwing a lively party around Thanksgiving that year involving a wide variety of games. Guests added a cranberry to their red ribbons every time they won a game. A cute anecdote points out that the 20th Century Club charter was, at some point, amended to ensure that members over 70 years of age would never be asked to keep the books. The 20th Century Club was later credited with bringing the game of bridge to San Angelo in the 1920s. Bridge was a pastime that my mother continued throughout her social life in San Angelo.

I only knew Gran through the stories mother told and the photos on the wall. She had already had a severe stroke and was bedridden when I was born in 1955. She died in 1960. I felt such gratitude to know that she was able to be present for that day of recognition in 1951.

Frank and Ralph Harris were generous supporters of Theodore Roosevelt's run for the presidency. But they both became disillusioned when Roosevelt instituted the Inheritance Tax. They were further incensed when the U.S. government initiated a program of destroying cattle to stabilize that commodity's financial markets. Some years later, however, Ralph Harris was named head of a committee to establish a Federal Land Bank in Texas. This was a governmental appointment and must have been some kind of favor from Roosevelt. He and Sadie moved to Houston temporarily for Ralph to tend to the project.

My Great Uncle Ledyard took on a larger than life stature, mostly from the way my mother talked about him and partly because he died young. He was an intelligent man with ambitions far beyond the plains of Texas and the ranching business. But his father insisted he raise cattle and probably even went to some lengths to get Ledyard started in the business. Perhaps because his ambition was squelched or perhaps because he had the misfortune to inherit the Harris family alcoholism genes, Ledyard quickly became unable to control his drinking. By his late twenties, in the advanced stages of his illness, he could no longer care for himself. His siblings picked up the responsibility for him but in the end it was my Nana, Helen Harris Weaver, who sent him five dollars each week to pay his rent and have some spending money. Any more money and the bums on the street would just roll him and take it. He died at age 31.

In May of 1923, oil was discovered on the Harris land and the already successful families were, I imagine, catapulted into even greater assets. Ralph Harris bought additional property in Coke County. Nana--Helen Harris Weaver, inherited it when Ralph died in 1948 and ranched it along with the original Harris brothers' "Headquarters" Ranch throughout World War II. All of that land passed to my mother, Helen, and my Aunt Sadie Gwin when Nana was killed.

Ralph and Sadie's daughter, Helen Harris (Nana), grew into quite a beauty. In about 1921, at age 17 or 18, she posed for pictures in her role as "Duchess of West Texas" at a debutante kind of festivity in Waco, Texas. She smiles at me from the series of three pictures taken of her wearing a sequined gown and looking out over a matching sequined fan. The fan hangs on the wall nearby, a little tattered and broken in several places. The tilt of this young woman's head and her quiet smile give a tantalizing impression of a sweet, but coy, young lady. She looks strikingly like her own mother as a young woman but the dress and hair suggest a later era. And my aunt has told me about Nana and the festival in Waco. Two years later, Helen Harris married and became Helen Harris Allen, wife of Harvey Hicks Allen from Temple, Texas.

Sadie Gwin and Helen were both born in San Angelo—my aunt, Sadie Gwin, in 1924 and my mother, Helen, in 1927. Helen, at least, was born in the Clinic Hospital, across the street from the house that Ralph and Sadie Harris built on Beauregard Street in about 1920.

Endnotes

"Quote me as saying I was misquoted."
~ Groucho Marx

Chapter One

1   San Angelo Standard Times. 20 Jan. 1955: A1. Print.
2   Houston Post. 26 Feb. 1955: A1+. Print.
3   San Angelo Standard Times. 20 Jan. 1955: A1. Print.
4   Ibid.
5   San Angelo Standard Times. 11 Feb. 1955. A1+. Print.
6   San Angelo Standard Times. 20 Jan. 1955: A1. Print.
7   Ibid.
8   Ibid.
9   North, Joe. Telephone Interview, estimated date, March, 1998.
10 San Angelo Standard Times. 20 Jan. 1955: A1+. Print.
11 Ibid.
12 Ibid.
13 Houston Post. 20 Jan. 1955: A1. Print.
14 San Angelo Standard Times. 20 Jan. 1955: A1+. Print.
15 Ibid.
16 Ibid.
17 Ibid.

Chapter Two

18 Ibid.
19 Ibid.
20 San Angelo Standard Times. 20 Jan. 1955: A11. Print.
21 Ibid.
22 Ibid.
23 Ibid.
24 Ibid.
25 San Angelo Standard Times. 21 Jan. 1955: A1. Print.

26 San Angelo Standard Times. 21 Jan. 1955: A1+. Print.
27 Houston Post. 21 Jan. 1955: A1+. Print.
28 Ibid.
29 San Angelo Standard Times. 23 Jan. 1955: A1. Print.
30 Ibid.
31 San Angelo Standard Times. 23 Jan. 1955: A1. Print.
32 San Angelo Standard Times. 24 Jan. 1955: A1. Print.
33 Ibid.
34 Ibid.
35 Houston Post. 21 Jan. 1955: A1. Print.
36 San Angelo Standard Times. 23 Jan. 1955. A1. Print.
37 San Angelo Standard Times. 25 Jan. 1955. A1. Print.
38 Houston Post. 27 Jan. 1955: A1+. Print.
39 Houston Post. 24 Jan. 1955: A1. Print.
40 Ibid.
41 Ibid.
42 Houston Post. 26 Jan. 1955: A1. Print.
43 Ibid.
44 Ibid.
45 San Angelo Standard Times. 27 Jan. 1955. A1. Print.
46 Ibid.
47 Ibid.
48 Ibid.
49 Ibid.
50 San Angelo Standard Times. 27 Jan. 1955. A1. Print.
51 Ibid.
52 Ibid.
53 Houston Post. 28 Jan. 1955: A1. Print.
54 Ibid.
55 Ibid.
56 Houston Post. 28 Jan. 1955: A1+. Print.
57 Ibid.
58 Ibid.
59 Ibid.
60 Houston Post. 29 Jan. 1955: A1. Print.
61 Ibid.
62 Ibid.
63 Ibid.
64 Houston Post. 30 Jan. 1955: A1+. Print.
65 Ibid.
66 San Angelo Standard Times. 13 Feb. 1955. A1. Print.
67 Houston Post. 30 Jan. 1955: A1+. Print.
68 Ibid.

[69] Telephone conversation. Estimated date March of 1998.
[70] Houston Post. 30 Jan. 1955: A1+. Print.
[71] San Angelo Standard Times. 3 Feb. 1955. A1+. Print.

Chapter Three

[72] San Angelo Standard Times. 3 Feb. 1955. A1+. Print.
[73] San Angelo Standard Times. 2 Feb. 1955. A1+. Print.
[74] San Angelo Standard Times. 3 Feb. 1955. A1+. Print.
[75] Ibid.
[76] Ibid.
[77] Ibid.
[78] San Angelo Standard Times. 4 Feb. 1955. A1. Print.
[79] Ibid.
[80] Ibid.
[81] Ibid.
[82] Ibid.
[83] Ibid.
[84] Ibid.
[85] San Angelo Standard Times. 6 Feb. 1955. A1. Print.
[86] Ibid.
[87] Ibid.
[88] San Angelo Standard Times. 6 Feb. 1955. A1. Print.
[89] Blackburn, Edward A., Jr. *Wanted: Historic Jails of Texas.* College Station. Texas A & M University Press. p 324.
[90] San Angelo Standard Times. 9 Feb. 1955. A1. Print.
[91] San Angelo Standard Times. 11 Feb. 1955. A1. Print.
[92] Ibid.
[93] Ibid.
[94] Ibid.
[95] Ibid.
[96] Ibid.
[97] San Angelo Standard Times. 12 Feb. 1955. A1. Print.
[98] Ibid.
[99] Ibid.
[100] San Angelo Standard Times. 13 Feb. 1955. A1. Print.
[101] Ibid.
[102] Ibid.
[103] Ibid.
[104] Ibid.
[105] Ibid.
[106] Ibid.
[107] Ibid.
[108] Ibid.

109 Ibid.

110 Ibid.

111 Ibid.

112 Ibid.

113 Ibid.

114 San Angelo Standard Times. 16 Feb. 1955. A1. Print.

115 Ibid.

116 Thaler, Paul. *The Watchful Eye. American Justice in the Age of the Television Trial.* Westport, London. Praeger Press. p. xix.

Chapter Four

117 Houston Post. 30 Jan. 1955: A1+. Print.

118 Ibid.

119 Houston Post. 30 Jan. 1955: A1+. Print.

120 Ibid.

Chapter Five

121 The U.S. Food and Drug Administration currently labels Valium as a Pregnancy Category D pharmaceutical. This means there is "positive evidence of human fetal risk based on adverse reaction data from investigational or marketing experience or studies in humans, but potential benefits may warrant the use of the drug in pregnant women despite potential risks." Source: Wikipedia.

122 Worden, J. William. *Grief Counseling and Grief Therapy.* 2nd Edition. Springer Publishing. New York. 1981.

Chapter Six

123 www. Bartleby .com J.F. Kennedy Inaugural Address.

124 Bradshaw, John. *On: The Family.* Health Communications, Inc. Deerfield Beach, FA 1988.

Chapter Eight

125 Bradshaw, John. *On: The Family.* Health Communications, Inc. Deerfield Beach, FA 1988.

Chapter Sixteen

126 Reverend Faith Moran. Est date October 2005

Chapter Eighteen

127 Wilson, James L. *Adrenal Fatigue: The 21st Century Stress Syndrome.* Smart Publications. Petaluma.

128 Wikipedia, Cortisol.

About the Author

Tess Keehn received her Master of Counseling degree in 1994. She recently retired from a 20-year career as a licensed mental health professional, most recently in the department of psychiatry of a health maintenance organization.

Confronted with the aftermath of a family tragedy that occurred prior to her birth, Tess dedicated herself, as a young adult, to finding emotional balance and wellness. Prior to becoming a qualified mental health caregiver, Tess began to heal her wounds through psychotherapy and her pursuit of spiritual awakening. Empowered by wisdom and insights gained in a wide variety of new thought and interfaith settings as well as alternative care for the mind, body and spirit, Tess offers Alchemical Inheritance – some highlights of that most personal journey - for your benefit.

Tess paints with words and also enjoys painting with watercolors. She lives with her (amazing!) husband, Michael, near Sacramento, California. She cherishes time with her extended family, spiritual family and in various volunteer capacities.

Tess provides self-empowerment life coaching on a part-time basis to select clients, often by telephone. Find out more at Alchemicalinheritance.com or YourWiseMind.com.

Printed in the United States
By Bookmasters